SMOKED

SMOKED

HOW TO CURE & PREPARE MEAT, SEAFOOD, VEGETABLES, FRUIT & MORE

JEREMY SCHMID

PHOTOGRAPHY BY DEVIN HART

CONTENTS

INTRODUCTION

I have always enjoyed the taste of smoked foods – when you make your own sausages and charcuterie as I do, there is a big call for their subsequent smoking. I've included some of my most successful recipes and methods, which I hope will inspire you as you develop your own skills, and experience the satisfying nuances of taste produced by smoked foods.

I was introduced to smoking food early in my cooking career. In many of the establishments where I have worked, at home and overseas, there has been a strong focus on smoked ingredients for creating specific tastes; in turn, this gave these restaurants a talking point as they were doing something different with food. More than 15 years ago I bought a commercial smoker because of the diversity smoking can give to a variety of foods. Most importantly I enjoy both the process of smoking and the subtlety of character produced by bringing this new element to a dish.

The practice of smoking food was probably born from the happy chance of cavemen leaving fresh pieces of meat hanging in the path of the smoke from their fire! In many countries and for many generations the smoking process has been used as an easy way to preserve food for storage. Once salt began to be traded, and became more available, people started to use this ingredient to 'cure' meats first in order to preserve them and then smoke them to help prolong their shelf life. For centuries the only way for some civilisations to preserve foods was by heavily salting and smoking them. These methods lost popularity with the advent of refrigeration and the convenience of supermarkets with their large refrigerated and frozen food sections. Recently, however, the interest in different types of food preparation has increased hugely. (Cooking competitions on the television along with whole channels being dedicated to cooking programmes, making it possible to watch food TV all day and every day, reflect this.) We now smoke food for the taste and to connect with tradition.

So far have we moved away from these early preservation methods that until relatively recently the art of smoking food was looked on as the exclusive domain of hunters and fishers, done primarily to preserve some of the hunt or catch to eat at a later occasion. The possibilities of smoking are, however, by no means limited to the preservation of meat and fish; there are endless different tastes to be achieved with many – some unexpected – types of food. Even some very simple methods of smoking can alter and enhance taste in surprising ways. The final tone produced by smoking also has visual appeal and adds to the end result.

The amount of money and time required to successfully make smoked products can initially be minimal, but should you develop a keen interest you may want to construct or buy a more permanent smoker. You could also team up with one or two friends to share the cost and use the activity as an excuse for a get-together!

Smoking food is an experience too, and I have fond memories of the time when I took a break from cooking in restaurants and leased a property specifically to make sausages and hams. Sometimes local hunters and fishers would turn up and ask me to brine and cure their catch for them. Once my facility became known in the area, visits became more social often leading to a yarn or two being shared around the smoker.

I hope that my recipes will bring you the same pleasure they have given me.

THE SMOKING PROCESS

SMOKING ENHANCES THE TASTE OF A GREAT VARIETY OF FOODS, FROM DAIRY PRODUCTS SUCH AS BUTTER, CREAM AND CHEESE, TO MEATS AND FISH, OR VEGETABLES SUCH AS TOMATOES, EGGPLANT AND ONIONS. EVEN SPICES SUCH AS SALT, PEPPER AND PAPRIKA CAN BE SMOKED, AS CAN CEREAL GRAINS BEFORE THEY ARE USED TO MAKE BEER.

The process of smoking food can be broken down into two methods: hot and cold smoking. Generally a chamber temperature less than 30°C/85°F is considered cold, that is, where the smoking process does not 'cook' the food.

Cold smoking includes first curing meat or seafood in a salt and sugar blend, allowing some of the moisture to be extracted from the flesh, which helps prevent bacterial growth and lets the salt permeate the product, contributing to its preservation and taste.

With hot smoking, the food is cooked by the heat of the smoker and typically it will be ready to eat once the process is complete. Meats need to be brined, meaning soaked for a period of time in a cold salt water solution, before hot smoking to bring out texture and taste. You can also brine fish and seafood, if you wish. The chamber temperatures for hot smoking range from between 50°C/122°F and 80°C/176°F, and up to 90°C/194°F.

The alternative to traditional smoking is the use of liquid smoke. This is smoke that has been condensed into a liquid form, usually with the addition of water. Liquid smoke is commonly used in large production plants for reasons of cost, or if there is not the space or time for traditional methods. This method steeps the food with a smoke essence and no smoking takes place; your product will have a smoked taste but without the preferred tint gained through the actual smoking process. Liquid smoke can be used prior to cooking, for instance lightly brushed onto scallops before searing or mixed into cream when making a smoked potato gratin.

With both hot and cold smoking, the product needs to have a dry surface before it is smoked; this will help with the final hue and the product will infuse the smoke taste better than if it is wet.

With any smoking method the type of smoker you have and the fuel you use in the smoker will affect the taste and outcomes. Writing down what you have done each time and the qualities of the finished food means you can always refer back to a particular recipe and adjust it in future if you wish to achieve different results.

The tastes you can achieve with smoking food predominantly come from the fuel you use. Wood chips are a significant fuel for smoking. Some woods lend themselves to certain meats and a blend of different woods can bring excellent results. It's worth noting that wherever you are in the world, there will be locally sourced wood chips from different tree species available to try. For example, when smoking chicken you could try adding cherry wood to your choice of wood, if available. This creates a finished product that is light and sweet. When smoking pork, the addition of some chipped wine barrel oak with straight oak can add sweetness from the wine residue, which would not be present from just the oak chips.

It is also possible to smoke with other fuels such as tea and hay, and spices can also be added to add tang (see alternative fuels page 18).

→ HOT SMOKING

Hot smoking is the easiest form of smoking and you will quickly get a finished product that can be consumed straightaway, stored, or used in another recipe. Hot smoking is a great method to use for meats such as hams, pastrami and sausages.

Before smoking, meat and seafood need to be brined, meaning cured, 'rubbed' or marinated before hot smoking. Vegetables and fruit do not need to be brined, though can be if you want to add other tastes, for instance salting eggplant (aubergine) before smoking. Making a light sugar solution and soaking apples before smoking will prevent them from going brown and sweeten them.

The hot smoking process does not lend itself to dairy products since the heat changes the fats and softens or melts the product to such a degree that it is no longer usable. Obviously it is a waste of time to hot smoke butter as it will become a melted mess in your smoker!

Many vegetables such as onions, tomatoes, capsicums (bell peppers), corn and sweet potatoes (kumara) take on pleasant additional aromas after hot smoking, which can enhance your finished dish.

During the smoking process the heat in the smoking chamber will reach temperatures greater than 40°C/104°F, at which point the foods will start to cook. Some foods will require a longer smoking or cooking time than others. For example, a ham needs to reach an internal temperature of 72°C/162°F, which might take up to 10 hours, whereas a side of salmon may only take 20 minutes. At completion of the smoking process the hot smoked meat will be ready to eat or can stored in the refrigerator once cooled.

With fish, hot smoking can be the quickest way to enjoy your catch. Taking a couple of fillets, such as salmon or snapper, lightly seasoning them with salt and placing a thin layer of brown sugar on the fillets then smoking them until cooked usually takes no more than 20 minutes – this is a simple way to enjoy freshly smoked fish. Salmon, tuna, mackerel and marlin are also ideal for this process.

All types of wood work well with the hot smoking process. It is possible to use a single type of wood or a blend of two or three varieties. Adding other materials such as tea or hay can also work very well and give quite different hints to the usual wood smoke.

→ COLD SMOKING

The process of cold smoking generally takes longer than hot smoking but the results are worth it; cold smoking times may vary from hours to several days. Cold smoking helps to preserve the product and allows for longer storage; it was traditionally done for this reason. In most cases the process begins with curing.

One of the most important things to remember with cold smoking is that it is necessary for the smoke to be cold when it comes into contact with the food you are preparing. Some types of smokers will make this process easier than others, but crucially you do not want to 'cook' the product you are preparing. You want to keep the integrity of the original product, for instance butter should not melt, although it will usually get a little soft, salmon should not cook and cream should not heat up. Once the items are removed from the smoker they should still be cool and not warm or hot.

To cold smoke foodstuffs you need to have the heat source and smoke some distance away from the food being smoked so that when the smoke comes into contact with the food it will have lost most or all of its heat. An easy way to achieve this is to have the heat source outside the smoking chamber and to flow the smoke through a tube connected to the chamber. Alternatively you can place a tray of ice between the heat source and the product; this will both cool the chamber and help prevent the heat rising and cooking the food being smoked.

Smoked air-dried bacon is an example of a meat that has been cold smoked. You can eat the finished bacon 'raw', after it has been cured, smoked and air dried or you can cook it. When cooked, this style of bacon becomes crispy, just like the bacon from your childhood. Various beef, pork and venison cuts, once cured, respond very well to the cold smoking process.

Cold smoked fish, such as salmon, trout and other oily fish, can be eaten without being cooked. The process begins by curing the fish in a salt and sugar mix or salt brine, then once it has been dried and smoked, it is ready to eat.

Cold smoking is the method of choice for dairy products. You can achieve very fine results with various cheeses, from semi-soft styles such as Brie to harder types like Cheddar. Butter and cream can also be successfully cold smoked.

Vegetables such as tomatoes and onions can be cold smoked. Temperatures may vary according to what is being smoked. With protein-rich foods such as meat, fish and cheese, the temperature must stay below 30°C/86°F because at temperatures over 40°C/104°F the protein will start to cook. With vegetables there is a greater degree of tolerance, which is why I have indicated higher temperatures when cold smoking these items.

The wood chips used in cold smoking are the same as in hot smoking. My preference is to use the lighter woods or a blend, as generally this method needs a longer period of smoke time. The lighter woods have a subtler aroma so if you like a stronger smoke try blending lighter woods with stronger ones.

Cold smoking begins with a curing process, where salt, sugar and othe ingredients are added to the product, usually in the form of a dry mix without the addition of water. Curing helps to draw out water from the item and to preserve it before smoking. It can take from two days to five weeks or more depending on the size and type of item you wish to smoke. I cure delicate proteins such as salmon in a salt and sugar mix for two days, whereas if I am preparing a beef eye or round from the back leg of the animal I will cure it for five weeks before smoking. For dairy products, such as cheese and cream, I cold smoke these without any initial process.

→ LIQUID SMOKE

Although not technically a smoking process, liquid smoke is the easiest way to get a smoked essence into food; however, you will be limited by the variety available, with hickory being the most common. This method basically uses an added taste that comes in liquid form. It can be added to the brine when curing meats such as pastrami, bacon or chicken. Once cured, these meats are then cooked, which gives them a smoked taste. Other ingredients that can be given the liquid smoke treatment are cream, scallops and sauces. By softening butter, adding a little liquid smoke then whipping it lightly, you can quickly make smoked butter. Be aware that the results of liquid smoking will be similar to a standard bought product, and will lack the individual notes and tints you get from traditional smoking. The tastes do tend to be quite strong, so using the recommended amount of liquid smoke is essential.

SMOKING UNITS

There are many different types of smokers available in a wide range of sizes and prices. Deciding what you intend to smoke is the simplest way of choosing a smoker that is best for you and your needs. If, for instance, you only want to hot smoke small items then a small stove top smoker will be adequate. If you would like to smoke whole legs of ham, large cuts of meat or a large volume of food then you may want to consider making a smoker from a wine barrel, a 44-gallon (200-litre) drum or building one from scratch. For most situations in between, there are smokers available from your local appliance, hardware or outdoor living store. A smoking chamber should obviously have no large holes, be set up for holding some type of rack system on which to place the food, and be cleanable.

→ STOVE TOP SMOKERS

Stove top smoker are perfect for smoking small items. This is the easiest way to start smoking food. Recipes such as the hot smoked fish (see page 62) and hot smoked venison loin (see page 28) use this method with excellent results. Although there are many types of these basic smokers on the market, you can make your own with equipment you probably already have without having to purchase anything more than a bag of smoking sawdust or chips. In most commercial kitchens a stove top smoker often consists of a stainless steel tray with 15–20 cm (6–8 in) sides, large enough to hold a cake rack (see opposite and page 62–63).

To prepare your stove top smoker, place the fine smoking chips or sawdust in the base of the tray. Place the tray on the element or heat source. Start with a high heat until smoke is created and then turn down the heat to low, allowing the sawdust or chips to smoulder and smoke without catching fire. If the sawdust catches fire the smoked food will have a burnt and bitter taste. Place the cake rack with the item to

be smoked over the smoking chips ensuring there is a ¾–1¼ in (2–3 cm) gap between the rack and the chips or sawdust. Finally cover the whole tray with aluminium foil. I like to get the smoker going before adding the item to be smoked as this helps to control the smoke; if you have the smoker all covered and then start the heat, you will inevitably take a peek when it starts smoking.

You will need to change the sawdust every 20–30 minutes as it will usually only smoke for this length of time. After the smoking process is complete, remove the tray from the heat and allow it to stand for a few minutes before removing the foil and enjoying the results.

Remember to be careful when removing the foil as this can set off your smoke alarm if you are indoors!

→ LARGER HOT SMOKING UNITS

From a basic stove top method you can progress to a larger hot smoker with which you can control the internal temperature of the chamber. These usually self-feeding units continuously add more wood chips or pellets to the heat source and have the ability to smoke items for times ranging from minutes to hours. This type of smoker may need specially-made wood pellets to operate, which can be an extra expense, but they do offer consistent results and are both easy to set up and to use. These can be found at hunting and fishing stores, online or at specialist barbecue stores.

→ COLD SMOKING UNITS

There are now smoking units that can do both hot and cold smoking or just cold smoking. One of the simplest and cheapest cold smoking units consists of a stainless steel cylinder in which smoke is generated and then blown by an aquarium pump through a protruding tube inserted into a smoking chamber. These can be attached to most chambers such as a wooden wine barrel, a barbecue with a lid, or any type of chamber suitable for holding smoke for a longer period of time.

An alternative way of cold smoking is to put some form of cooling between the heat source and the product in a larger hot smoker. In some smokers it is possible to place a stainless steel tray full of ice as close as possible to the wood chips or sawdust without affecting the smoking process. This cools the smoke and when the smoke rises it has a lot less heat and the food and chamber are kept cold. This will only work until the ice melts of course! This kind of smoker will require a little more attention but can create good results at inexpensive cost.

Or, you could have the heat source outside the smoking chamber and flow the smoke through a pipe into the chamber. If the distance between the two is great enough for the smoke to lose its heat, this can be a very effective form of cold smoking and allows the product to be smoked for a long time without heating the chamber.

COLD SMOKING

HOW TO MAKE A COLD SMOKER

1. YOU WILL NEED ONE WINE BARREL AND SOME TYPE OF SMOKE-PRODUCING SYSTEM. FOR THIS I HAVE USED A UNIT CALLED SMOKE GENERATOR.

2. ALL BANDS WILL NEED TO BE SCREWED IN PLACE. SCREW EACH PIECE OF WOOD TO THE BAND ON THE BASE AS WELL AS TO THE LID.

5. MAKE SURE ALL RODS ARE EVEN ON BOTH SIDES AND LEVEL.

6. ATTACH YOUR SMOKER FOLLOWING THE MANUFACTURER'S INSTRUCTIONS.

7. THE FINISHED WINE BARREL SMOKER.

3. CUT THE TOP OFF BETWEEN THE TWO TOP BANDS TO FORM A LID.

4. DRILL HOLES FROM THE OUTSIDE IN AND INSERT METAL RODS FOR PLACING DOWEL RODS OR WIRE RACKS. MARK WHERE THE ROD MEETS THE OTHER SIDE, AND DRILL PART OF THE WAY THROUGH FROM THE INSIDE OUT. PUSH THE ROD INTO PLACE; THIS MAY REQUIRE A LITTLE HAMMERING.

8. BE CAREFUL WHEN OPENING; IT'S BEST TO AVOID RELEASING A LARGE QUANTITY OF SMOKE AT ONE TIME.

9. CAREFULLY PLACE THE PRODUCT IN THE BARREL MAKING SURE IT HANGS FROM THE RODS IN THE SMOKER.

10. REMOVING THE SMOKED PRODUCT.

➡ WOOD & OTHER FUELS

Different woods create different effects in the finished smoked item. I really like to use lighter woods such as cherry or apple because I find these fruit woods give a slightly sweeter smoke than oak. You can buy these as chips or save the branches when you are pruning your fruit trees.

You can also experiment with mixing woods together to achieve different smoke characteristics. These 'mixed' woods are now readily available in stores that supply wood chips for smoking, although don't let this stop you from using your own blends.

It is really important that any wood you use is untreated and has not been painted or stained before it has been chipped; these materials will not only affect the taste of the food but the chemicals released when smoked will be harmful to your health. Woods that are NOT used for smoking are ones that contain a lot of resin or are soft woods such as pine, fir or cedar.

Soaking the chips in water or even some other liquid such as whisky or red wine (use alcohol without too much sugar content as this may caramelise and burn before the process begins) will help to generate more smoke. But check your manufacturer's recommendations first; some smokers are built to only take wooden pellets (wood chips compressed into discs) which are fed into the smoker on a timer. These smokers tend to be more expensive and will limit the types of wood you are able to use. Others require small wood chips about the size of a beer bottle cap and some use sawdust. For the best results follow the smoker manufacturer's recommendations.

WOOD	TASTE PROFILES
FRUIT WOODS	SWEET, LIGHT; PLEASANT BY THEMSELVES OR CAN BE BLENDED WITH APPLE, CHERRY, PEAR AND STRONGER WOODS
HICKORY	STRONG; GOOD BY ITSELF OR CAN ALSO BE BLENDED WITH FRUIT WOODS
MANUKA (TEA TREE)	STRONG, HEAVY; BLEND WITH FRUIT WOODS
OAK	STRONG, THOUGH NOT OVERPOWERING; GOOD BY ITSELF OR BLENDED WITH MAPLE
MESQUITE	VERY STRONG; GOOD TO BLEND WITH MAPLE OR FRUIT WOODS
MAPLE	SWEET, GOOD STAND-ALONE WOOD; USED LIKE FRUIT WOODS
WALNUT	STRONG, BEST BLENDED WITH LIGHTER WOODS

Manuka

Hickory

Mesquite

Cherry

Apple

Maple

→ ALTERNATIVE FUELS

While wood chips are the most common fuel for smoking, there are alternatives. For instance, you can use tea leaves, which can also be combined with various spices such as star anise, coriander or cumin.

The easiest way to smoke with tea leaves is to combine them with a little rice and brown sugar and then loosely wrap them with the food item to be smoked in a double layer of aluminium foil to form a parcel. Poke a few holes in the parcel with a carving fork and place it on top of the heat source of your smoker.

Using hay for an earthy smoked taste is typically English and works very well with lamb.

→→ OTHER EQUIPMENT

→ BRINE PUMP OR MEAT INJECTOR

These can resemble a bicycle pump or a large syringe and are used to pump brine into meat. A brine pump is used for brining large cuts of meat such as a whole pork leg, allowing the brine to get close to the bone and throughout all the meat, and speeding up the brining process. Smaller syringe-type injectors are suitable for pieces of bacon, chicken or any smaller cuts where you wish to inject brine or marinade.

A simple rule of thumb for size is: if the injector needle can reach the middle of the meat from both sides it should be long enough to brine or marinate the meat correctly. Injectors can be obtained from butchery suppliers, specialist barbecue shops, kitchen supply shops and some marinades even come with their own injectors that you can re-use.

Simply fill the pump or injector with the brine and evenly inject the brine into the meat, making sure you get close to the bones if there are any. Then place the meat into the brine to soak for the desired time (see page 23).

→ MEAT THERMOMETER

A meat thermometer comes in handy when you need to know the final internal temperature of a smoked or cooked product. They are especially useful for long, slow cooking processes.

→ DRYING CABINET

Once cured or smoked, some products such as sausages and larger cuts of meat can be air dried. For instance, after cold smoking bacon you can air dry it for up to three weeks in a drying cabinet. You will need a cabinet where the items can be hung and fanned gently with moving air to dry out, while at the same time protecting the products from any flying insects.

You can make your own cabinet by converting an old refrigerator, for instance, adapting the door to allow air to circulate in and out. Or, buy or make a cabinet with a fine mesh door and a fan system. The cabinet should have a rack system made from dowel, or similar, in order to suspend the food items freely. The drying products should not touch each other as you want to evenly dry the entire surface of the food.

→ MISCELLANEOUS

You will need a selection of chopping boards, good sharp knives and plastic containers with tight-fitting lids that fit into your refrigerator, as well as digital scales, a strainer, natural string, cling film (plastic wrap), a measuring jug (pitcher) and spoons, muslin, aluminium foil, wire mesh racks, metal hooks and kitchen scissors.

SMOKING MEATS

SOME ESSENTIAL GUIDELINES
AND AN INTRODUCTION TO THE
DELIGHTS OF SMOKED MEAT.

➤➤ HOT SMOKING MEATS

Here are some basic recipes for hot smoking meats that will ensure you get off to a good start. Do keep in mind that if you prefer different tastes or stronger smoke finishes, you can change or add ingredients to the brine as well as adjust the blend of wood or even lengthen the smoking time. I would encourage you to keep a record of the methods you use so that you can get the same results another time or change some aspects for a different outcome.

When hot smoking smaller cuts of meat such as tongue, venison loins, pork or chicken, apple, cherry and maple woods work well. In the case of larger joints and beef cuts such as brisket or eye of round, heavier more robust smoke tastes come into their own with the final products usually lending themselves to a stronger smoke.

→ BRINING

Hot smoked meats need to be brined before smoking. This will help with the taste and tenderness. You can alter the meats by adding different ingredients to the brines.

As with any brining process it is best practice to bring the brine to a boil and then fully cool it down before adding the meats. You can use the brining method for many different cuts of meats including any whole birds that you wish to smoke.

The size of the meat to be brined will make a difference to the brining time, and a brine pump will speed up the process. If you would like to make the recipes more quickly, a brine pump or meat injector is a good piece of equipment to have (see page 18).

BASIC BRINING RECIPES

BRINING RECIPE #1
1¾ pints (1 litre) water
1 tablespoon honey
2 tablespoons brown sugar
1 teaspoon coriander seeds
1¾ oz (50 g) salt
1 teaspoon pink curing salt (see glossary)
1 teaspoon black peppercorns
1 tablespoon pickling spice

Place all the ingredients in a large pan and bring to the boil. Remove from the heat and cool, then chill in the refrigerator before use.

BRINING RECIPE #2
1¾ pints (1 litre) water
1 teaspoon celery seeds
2 tablespoons flaky sea salt
1 tablespoon raw (demerara) sugar
1 small fresh lime, halved and juiced

Place all the ingredients in a pan and bring to the boil. Remove from the heat and cool, then chill in the refrigerator before use.

BASIC GUIDELINES FOR BRINING TIMES

MEAT CUT	UNPUMPED	PUMPED
WHOLE CHICKEN 4–4½ LB (1.8–2 KG)	4 DAYS	24 HOURS
CHICKEN OR DUCK BREAST 7–9 OZ (200–250 G)	2 DAYS	12 HOURS
BEEF CHUCK 6½ LB (3 KG)	10 DAYS	3 DAYS
BEEF BRISKET 2¼ LB (1 KG)	7 DAYS	2 DAYS
BEEF EYE OF ROUND 3¼ LB (1.5 KG)	8 DAYS	2 DAYS
PORK HOCK 1¾–2 LB (800–900 G)	10 DAYS	3 DAYS
PORK LEG WHOLE 13¼–15½ LB (6–7 KG)	28 DAYS	7 DAYS
PORK BELLY WHOLE 6½–8¾ LB (3–4 KG)	5 DAYS	2 DAYS
VENISON LOIN 1 LB 2 OZ (500 G)	4 DAYS	24 HOURS
BEEF OR VEAL TONGUE 1 LB 6 OZ–1 LB 8 OZ (600–800 G)	7 DAYS	2 DAYS

PASTRAMI

This smoked and seasoned beef is served in thin slices, looks quite similar to corned beef and is often found in delicatessens. Pastrami is particularly popular in sliders – a small sandwich served in a bun – and bagels. Cold, pastrami is ideal in sandwiches, while freshly smoked and cooked it is a great addition at a barbecue. The recipe below is for hot smoked pastrami. See pages 26-27 for step-by-step instructions for preparing cold smoked pastrami.

BRINE
2¼ lb (1 kg) beef brisket
1¾ pints (1 litre) brining recipe #2, chilled (see page 22)

COOKING RUB
3 oz (¾ cup/85 g) coarsely ground peppercorns
4 oz (1 cup/115 g) coarsely ground coriander seeds
2 teaspoons coarsely ground juniper berries
1 tablespoon sweet smoked paprika
1 teaspoon garlic powder

I like to use oak or hickory for smoking pastrami, but use the wood type you prefer. You will need enough wood or wood pellets for a 3-hour smoke.

Soak the beef in the brine following the guidelines on page 23.

Once soaked, rinse off the brine and pat the beef dry with paper towels. If you have time you can dry the beef overnight in the refrigerator. Combine the cooking rub ingredients and rub into the beef.

Once the smoker is producing smoke, place the brisket on a rack fat side down for 1 hour. Then turn the brisket fat side up and smoke for 1-2 hours in order to reach an internal temperature of 72°C/161°F.

Once smoked, wrap the brisket in 3 layers of aluminium foil and bake in the oven or smoker for 2-3 hours at 110°C/230°F/Gas mark ¼ until you achieve an internal temperature of 85°C/185°F. If using the stove top method complete the process in the oven as it is very difficult to achieve the even temperature needed to finish the pastrami with this type of smoker.

If your smoker does not have a temperature gauge you will need to check this with a probe thermometer from time to time to make sure the meat is at the correct temperature. If it is becoming too hot or not getting hot enough finish it in the oven as described above.

Once the brisket has reached the correct temperature remove the meat from the oven or smoker and allow to rest for approximately 20 minutes. Remove the foil, being careful not to spill any moisture.

Pastrami is excellent eaten warm. For storage, allow to cool then wrap in cling film (plastic wrap) or place in an airtight container in the refrigerator for up to 2 weeks.

→ PASTRAMI

USING COLD SMOKING METHOD

1. BEEF BRISKET TO BE CURED.

2. INJECT THE BRINE INTO THE MEAT, INJECTING EVENLY OVER THE WHOLE PIECE.

6. PLACE THE BRISKET IN THE SMOKER FOR 3–4 HOURS FOR COLD SMOKING (FOR HOT SMOKING FOLLOW THE TEMPERATURE GUIDE ON PAGE 24).

7. REMOVE THE BRISKET FROM THE SMOKER.

3. SOAK THE BRISKET IN THE BRINE AFTER INJECTING (SEE PAGE 23 FOR TIMES).

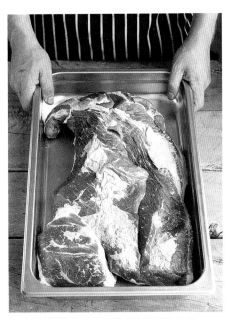

4. REMOVE THE BRISKET FROM THE BRINE AND PAT DRY.

5. LIBERALLY COAT THE BRISKET WITH THE COOKING RUB (SEE PAGE 24 FOR RECIPE).

8. WRAP THE BRISKET AND COOK IN THE OVEN FOR 4–5 HOURS UNTIL THE INTERNAL TEMPERATURE IS 85–90°C/185–194°F (FOR HOT SMOKING SEE PAGE 24).

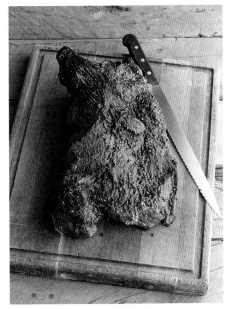

9. THE BRISKET CAN BE EATEN WARM, OR CHILLED AND SERVED COLD.

SMOKED CHICKEN

Everyone loves smoked chicken and this is an easy recipe to start making your own. First brine the chicken as this will help to keep it moist, soften the meat and give it taste. If you don't brine the meat you'll find that after the smoking and cooking process the meat is quite firm and dry.

4¼–4½ lb (1.9–2.1 kg) whole chicken
4½ pints (2.5 litres) brining recipe #1, chilled (see page 22)

Fruit wood gives excellent results with chicken. Use whatever wood you prefer. You will need enough wood or wood pellets for a 2-hour smoke.

Soak the fresh chicken in the chilled brine following the guidelines on page 23.

Remove from the brine, rinse under cold water then pat dry with paper towels. If you have time, you can dry the chicken overnight in the refrigerator.

Once the smoker is producing smoke, place the chicken on a rack in the smoker for approximately 2 hours until the internal temperature reaches 72°C. If your smoker does not get hot enough, bake the chicken in the oven for 1–1½ hours at 130–140°C until you achieve an internal temperature of 72°C/161°F. Check with a thermometer.

Once cooked through, remove the chicken from the oven and allow it to rest for 20–30 minutes before eating.

For storage, allow to cool then wrap in cling film (plastic wrap) and place in the refrigerator for up to 5 days.

HOT SMOKED VENISON LOIN

Venison loin is best eaten rare to medium-rare, so when hot smoking you only want it the internal temperature to be 50–60°C/122–140°F - although you can cook it to the temperature you wish. I find overcooked venison becomes dry.

1 lb 2 oz (500 g) venison loin
1¾ pints (1 litre) brining recipe #1, chilled (see page 22)
maple syrup, for brushing

Use whatever wood you prefer. You will need enough wood or wood pellets for a 1-hour smoke.

Soak the venison loin in the chilled brine following the guidelines on page 23.

Wash the venison lightly and pat dry with paper towels. If you have time, you can dry the venison overnight in the refrigerator. Lightly brush the loin with the maple syrup.

Once your smoker is producing smoke, place the venison loin on a rack in the smoker for 45 minutes–1 hour until the internal temperature reaches 50–60°C/122–140°F for rare to medium-rare. You should be able to get an internal temperature of 50–60°C on a stove top smoker after two gentle smokes.

Once smoked, remove the venison from the smoker and allow it to rest for 5–10 minutes before eating.

For storage, allow to cool then wrap in cling film (plastic wrap) and place in the refrigerator for up to 4 days.

SMOKED LAMB SHOULDER

This is a really tasty way of cooking lamb shoulder, great for those days when you are having friends around for a simple meal.

1 lamb shoulder, boned (approximately 2¼–3 lb (1–1.4 kg)
6 tablespoons rub #1 (see page 153)

I like to use a maple or apple wood blend for lamb but use whatever you prefer. You will need enough wood or wood pellets for a 2-hour smoke.

Put the opened lamb shoulder in a high-sided tray, sprinkle with the rub evenly on both sides and into any crevices then rest in the refrigerator for 2 hours.

Once your smoker is producing smoke, place the shoulder on a rack in the smoker for 2 hours.

Remove, wrap loosely in 2 layers of aluminium foil and cook in a preheated oven at 110°C/230°F/ Gas mark ¼ for about 3½-4½ hours or until it reaches an internal temperature of 85-90°C/185-194°F.

Once the shoulder is at the correct temperature, remove from the oven and allow to rest for approximately 20 minutes, then remove the aluminium foil, being careful to avoid spilling any moisture in the foil.

Lamb shoulder is excellent warm. For storage, allow to cool then wrap well in cling film (plastic wrap) and place in the refrigerator for up to 5 days.

SMOKED PORK SHOULDER

This is a great recipe to serve to a group of people. It takes a little while to cook but it's well worth the time.

1 boneless pork shoulder (approximately 6½ lb (3 kg)
10 tablespoons rub #2 (see page 153)

I like to use apple wood for this recipe but use whatever you prefer. You will need enough wood or wood pellets for a 2-hour smoke.

Place the pork shoulder onto a high-sided tray, sprinkle with the rub evenly on both sides and into any crevices and then rest in the refrigerator for 2 hours.

Once your smoker is producing smoke, place the pork on a rack in the smoker for 2 hours.

Remove, wrap loosely in 2 layers of aluminium foil and cook in a preheated oven at 110°C/230°F/ Gas mark ¼ for 4-4½ hours or until it reaches an internal temperature of 85°C/185°F.

Once the pork has reached the correct temperature, remove from the oven and allow to rest for 15-20 minutes, then remove carefully from the foil to avoid spilling any moisture left in the foil.

Smoked pork shoulder is best eaten warm. For storage, allow to cool, then wrap well in cling film (plastic wrap) and place in the refrigerator for up to 4 days.

HOT SMOKED BACON

This bacon is cured and then hot smoked so that you can eat it as soon as it's smoked. When it is chilled, you will find this bacon is easier to cut than cold smoked bacon (see page 38).

6½–8¾ lb (3–4 kg pork belly
10½ pints (6 litres) brining recipe #1, chilled (see page 22)

When making bacon I like to use maple and apple wood but use whatever you prefer. You will need enough wood or wood pellets for a 2-3 hour smoke.

Soak the pork belly in the brine following the guidelines on page 23.

Remove from the brine, wash and place in the refrigerator overnight to dry.

Once your smoker is producing smoke place the belly on a rack in the smoker for 2-3 hours until the internal temperature reaches around 80°C/176°F. The smoking time required will depend on your smoker but generally the longer the process the richer the taste. If using a stove top smoker, or if the pork does not reach the correct internal temperature after smoking, bake in the oven at 100°C/210°F/Gas mark ¼ or less, for 45-60 minutes until you get an internal temperature of 72°C/161°F.

Once cooked, allow to cool, wrap in cling film (plastic wrap) and store in an airtight container in the refrigerator for up to 2 weeks.

For the best presentation, use a slicing machine and, for easier slicing, semi-freeze the belly beforehand so it is firm. You can slice the belly with a sharp knife if you do not have a slicing machine but the meat will need to be chilled.

For longer storage, cut each belly into 3 or 4 pieces and wrap with cling film (plastic wrap) then freeze. Defrost overnight in the refrigerator when required.

→ SMOKED SAUSAGES

I HAVE ENJOYED MAKING SAUSAGES FOR A NUMBER OF YEARS AND HAVE WON A GREAT MANY MEDALS AND PRIZES FOR THEM OVER THE YEARS. SMOKED SAUSAGES ARE AMONG MY PREFERRED TYPE OF SAUSAGE AND CAN BE USED IN A VARIETY OF RECIPES FROM PIZZAS TO CASSEROLES AND MANY DISHES IN BETWEEN.

→ MAKING YOUR OWN SAUSAGES

During the sausage-making process it is very important to make sure the meat and the equipment are kept chilled the whole time. Always wash the equipment thoroughly after making the sausages, and clean it again before reusing.

PREPARING THE CASINGS TO HOLD THE MEAT

If you are using natural casings, soak these for 20 minutes and wash them out in cold water.

Run water through the inside of the casing before filling it, to ensure any salt is removed. This will also highlight any holes in the casing. If you discover a hole, cut the casing there and restart the washing out at the broken piece.

Once you have washed out one casing, place it into a container of fresh water, with one end hanging over the side to make it easy to pick up when filling the sausages. Repeat as necessary.

USING THE SAUSAGE FILLER

When putting the casing on the nozzle of a sausage filler, first wet the nozzle with a little cooking oil to make it easier to thread the casing on. Gently feed as much of the casing as possible onto the nozzle without tearing the casing.

To start filling the casing, wind the handle of the sausage filler so the mix is just protruding from the end of the nozzle. Pull the casing over the end of the nozzle and tie the end of the casing so all air is removed from inside the skin.

As you fill the sausage, hold the skin against the nozzle to control the flow of the meat, making sure the casing is well filled and has no air pockets. Use a needle to prick any air pockets that may have formed. Continue to fill the skin until no more mix is left in the filler. Cut the skin, leaving enough overlap of the casing to tie a final knot once you have linked the sausages. Do not tie this end until all sausages have been linked.

LINKING THE SAUSAGES

To link the sausages, make sure the first knot at the front end of the casing is well tied. Hold this end in your left hand, then move your left hand to about 4-5 in (12-14 cm) from the end. Gently squeeze your thumb and forefinger together without breaking the skin.

Move your right hand to about 4-5 in (12-14 cm) from your left hand and gently squeeze the sausage here, without breaking the skin. Gently twirl the sausage a few times between both hands. Repeat this process until the whole skin is linked.

SMOKED CHORIZO SAUSAGES

Chorizo sausages come in many forms and this is my take on this classic. I tend to make them mild but, by doubling the chilli content, you can increase the heat if you like them hot.

2¼ lb (1 kg) pork shoulder (skinless
  and boneless)
3½ oz (100 g) clean pork back fat
¾ tablespoon fine salt
2 teaspoons sugar
1 tablespoon sweet smoked paprika

½ teaspoon cayenne pepper
¼ teaspoon pink curing salt (see glossary)
1 garlic clove, crushed
¼ teaspoon ground black pepper
¼ teaspoon ground cloves
¼ teaspoon ground nutmeg

I like to use a fruit wood blend for chorizo but use whatever you prefer. You will need enough wood or wood pellets for a 2-hour smoke. You will have difficulty attaining a good result with a stove top smoker so I recommend a smoker with a chamber large enough to allow the sausages to hang inside without touching each other.

Cut the pork and back fat into cubes, mix with the other ingredients and leave to cure overnight.

The next day, mince through a medium or coarse plate. Fill into 1¼ in (32-34 mm) casings (see page 32), making each sausage about 6 oz (180 g). Hang the sausages carefully over a dowel rod and leave overnight in the refrigerator.

The following day, dry the skins in an oven or smoker for about 30 minutes at 60°C/140°F.

Once your smoker is producing smoke, place the sausages on a rack in the smoker for 2 hours until the internal temperature reaches 72°C/161°F. If they get too hot the fat will drip from the sausage which will result in a dry finished product.

Remove from the smoker and allow to cool, then wrap in cling film (plastic wrap) and store in an airtight container in the refrigerator for up to 8 days. They also freeze well.

SMOKED PORK SAUSAGES

My friend Craig asked me to develop a breakfast sausage, and this is the result.

2¼ lb (1 kg) pork shoulder (skinless
  and boneless)
3½ oz (100 g) clean pork back fat
2 teaspoons sugar
¾ tablespoon salt

½ teaspoon ground black pepper
1 teaspoon dried sage
½ teaspoon ground fennel seeds
¼ teaspoon ground nutmeg
¼ teaspoon pink curing salt (see glossary)

Follow the process for making smoked chorizo as above, using the same types of fuel.

Once smoked, allow to cool then wrap in cling film (plastic wrap) and store in an airtight container in the refrigerator for up to 8 days. They also freeze well.

→ SMOKED RIBS

BECAUSE RIBS ARE THINNER THAN OTHER CUTS OF MEAT THEY NEED TO BE SMOKED AND COOKED SLOWLY IN ORDER FOR THEM NOT TO DRY OUT.

LAMB RIBS

6 whole lamb rib slabs
½ cup rub #1 (see page 153)
8 fl oz (1 cup/250 ml) barbecue sauce (see page 152)

I like to use apple wood for lamb ribs but use whatever you prefer. You will need enough wood or wood pellets for a 2-hour smoke.

Trim the ribs of any excess fat and remove the membrane from the bone side of the ribs. Season the ribs with the rub using two-thirds on the meat side and one-third on the bone side. Place on an oven tray and marinate for 30 minutes in the refrigerator.

Once your smoker is producing smoke, place the ribs on a rack in the smoker for 2 hours or until the chamber reaches a temperature of 80°C/176°F.

When the chamber is at the correct temperature remove the ribs from the smoker and divide into 3 portions of 2 slabs of ribs side by side, and place each portion onto a large sheet of aluminium foil. Brush the ribs with two-thirds of the barbecue sauce and lightly wrap them in the foil to allow steam to be released during the cooking process.

Place the 3 packets of foil-wrapped ribs on the tray and cook in the oven at 130°C/265°F/Gas mark ¾ for another 1½–2 hours or until tender. To check for tenderness, insert the sharp end of a bamboo skewer into the meat. There should be little resistance. If necessary return to the oven until cooked to your satisfaction. Once fully cooked, remove the ribs from the oven then turn the temperature up to 170°C/340°F/Gas mark 3½. Unwrap the ribs and return them to the tray, brush with the remaining barbecue sauce and bake for another 10–15 minutes until brown and caramelised – sticky and tasty just as they should be.

Divide and cut as you prefer and serve hot.

PORK RIBS

2 whole pork rib slabs
½ cup rub #2 (see page 153)
8 fl oz (1 cup/250 ml) barbecue sauce (see page 152)

I like to use maple wood for pork ribs but use whatever you prefer. You will need enough wood or wood pellets for a 2-hour smoke.

Trim the ribs of any excess fat and remove the membrane from the bone side of the ribs. Season the ribs with the rub using two-thirds on the meat side and one-third on the bone side. Place on an oven tray and marinate for 30 minutes in the refrigerator.

Once your smoker is producing smoke, place the ribs on a rack in the smoker for 2 hours or until the chamber reaches a temperature of 80°C/176°F.

When the chamber is at the correct temperature remove the ribs from the smoker and place each slab onto a large sheet of aluminium foil. Brush the ribs with two-thirds of the barbecue sauce and lightly wrap them in the foil to allow steam to be released during the cooking process.

Place the foil-wrapped ribs on the tray and bake in the oven at 130°C/265°F/Gas mark ¾ for another 1½-2 hours, or until tender. To check for tenderness, insert the sharp end of a bamboo skewer into the meat. There should be little resistance. If necessary return to the oven until cooked to your satisfaction. Once fully cooked, remove the ribs from the oven then turn the temperature up to 170°C/340°F/Gas mark 3½. Unwrap the ribs and return them to the tray, brush with the remaining barbecue sauce and bake for another 10-15 minutes, until brown and caramelised – sticky and tasty just how we like them.

Cut into 2-rib pieces and serve hot.

BEEF RIBS

2 short beef rib racks
½ cup rub #2 (see page 153)
8 fl oz (1 cup/250 ml) barbecue sauce (see page 152)

I like to use half hickory half apple wood for beef ribs but use whatever you prefer. You will need enough wood or wood pellets for a 2-hour smoke.

Trim the ribs of any excess fat and remove the membrane from the bone side of the ribs. Season the ribs with the rub using two-thirds on the meat side and one-third on the bone side. Place on an oven tray and marinate for 30 minutes in the refrigerator.

Once your smoker is producing smoke, place the ribs on a rack in the smoker for 2 hours or until the chamber reaches a temperature of 80°C/176°F.

When the chamber is at the correct temperature remove the ribs from the smoker and place each of the slabs onto a large sheet of aluminium foil. Brush the ribs with two-thirds of the barbecue sauce and lightly wrap them in the foil to allow steam to be released during the cooking process.

Place the 2 packets of foil-wrapped ribs on a tray and bake in the oven at 130°C/265°F/Gas mark ¾ for another 2½-2 hours, or until tender. To check for tenderness, insert the sharp end of a bamboo skewer into the meat. There should be little resistance. If necessary return to the oven until cooked to your satisfaction. Once fully cooked, remove the ribs from the oven then turn the temperature up to 170°C/340°F/Gas mark 3½. Unwrap the ribs and return them to the tray, brush with the remaining barbecue sauce and bake for another 10-15 minutes until brown and caramelised – making the ribs sticky and extra tasty. Cut into individual ribs and serve hot.

COLD SMOKING MEATS

THERE ARE A FEW DIFFERENT METHODS OF COLD SMOKING MEATS. SOME RECIPES START WITH A CURING PROCESS THEN GO ON TO SMOKING AND SUBSEQUENT DRYING, WHILE OTHERS JUST USE A CURE OR MARINADE AND COLD SMOKING WITH THE SMOKED PRODUCT REQUIRING COOKING AFTERWARDS. THE MEATS IN THESE RECIPES WILL NEED TO BE COOKED BEFORE EATING.

SMOKED HAM HOCK

Smoked ham hocks can form part of a great winter meal. They can also add plenty of depth and provide a lot of meat to soups and stews. After smoking, the hocks can be frozen and used later at a time when you want something hearty to enjoy on a cold night.

4 ham hocks
7 pints (4 litres) brining recipe #1, chilled (see page 22)

Use whatever wood you prefer. You will need enough wood or wood pellets for a 2-3-hour smoke.

Soak the hocks in the chilled brine following the guidelines on page 23.

Remove from the brine, rinse and pat dry with paper towels. Place in the refrigerator overnight to dry.

Once your smoker is producing smoke, place the hocks on a rack in the smoker for 2-3 hours, ensuring the chamber temperature remains under 40°C/104°F for the entire time.

Remove, allow to cool then wrap in cling film (plastic wrap) and store in an airtight container in the refrigerator for up to 4 days.

SMOKED VEAL TONGUE

2 x 1 lb 6 oz–1 lb 9 oz (600–700 g) veal tongues
3½ pints (2 litres) brining recipe #1, chilled (see page 22)

Use whatever wood you prefer. You will need enough wood or wood pellets for a 2-3-hour smoke.

Soak the tongues in the chilled brine following the guidelines on page 23. Remove from the brine, rinse and pat dry with paper towels. Place in the refrigerator overnight to dry.

Once your smoker is producing smoke, place the tongues on a rack in the smoker for 2-3 hours, ensuring the chamber temperature remains less than 40°C/104°F for the entire time.

Remove, allow to cool then wrap in cling film (plastic wrap) and store in an airtight container in the refrigerator for up to 4 days. Tongue can be frozen.

SMOKED CHICKEN & HERB SAUSAGES

Smoked chicken is always a popular food. It is possible to make smoked sausages by marinating and cold smoking the meat before mincing it and making it into sausages. This gives the sausages a nice smoked taste but they look like fresh unsmoked sausages. It can be interesting watching people's reactions when they taste these sausages as they won't be expecting their tasty smoked accents. These are fantastic on the barbecue – and quick because they are precooked so just need to be heated through.

2¼ lb (1 kg) chicken (14 oz/400 g skinless breast meat and 1 lb 6 oz/600 g skin-on thigh meat)
¾ tablespoon fine salt
1 teasoon sugar
¼ teaspoon ground white pepper
1 garlic clove, crushed

¼ teaspoon dried thyme
3 fl oz (90 ml) chilled water or 3¼ oz (90 g) crushed ice
1 tablespoon fresh chopped herbs (such as parsley and chives)

I like to use apple wood for this recipe but use what you prefer. Make sure you have sufficient wood or wood pellets for a 1–2-hour smoke.

Marinate the chicken meat with the salt, sugar, pepper, garlic and dried thyme for at least a few hours, or overnight in the refrigerator for the best taste.

Once your smoker is producing smoke, put the marinated chicken meat on a tray and place in the smoker for 1–2 hours, ensuring the chamber temperature remains under 20°C/68°F for the entire time the meat is in the smoker.

Once the meat is smoked, return it to the refrigerator for 1 hour.

Mince (grind) the meat through a medium plate into a large bowl or deep tray. Place about a quarter of the mixture into a food processor and then add the water or ice and blend to a fine paste. If your food processor is not large enough you may need to do this in smaller batches. Return the paste to the rest of the minced meat and add the fresh chopped herbs. Mix by hand or in an electric mixer with a paddle attachment on low speed until well combined.

Fill into 1¼ in (30–32 mm) casings (see page 32), making each sausage approximately about 6 oz (180 g).

COLD SMOKED BACON

This can be used like pancetta, although it is smoked. Try wrapping cold smoked bacon around chicken breast, eye fillet (tenderloin), beans and asparagus before cooking. Unlike hot smoked bacon (see page 30), which can be eaten as is or cooked, cold smoked bacon will require cooking before eating.

6½–8¾ lb (3–4 kg) pork belly
10½ pints (6 litres) brining recipe #1, chilled (see page 22)

I like to use a blend of half maple and apple wood but use whatever you prefer. You will need enough wood or wood pellets for a 2–6-hour smoke.

Soak the pork belly in the brine in a large container following the guidelines on page 23.

Remove from the brine, rinse and pat dry with paper towels. Place in the refrigerator overnight to dry.

Once your smoker is producing smoke, place the belly on a rack in the smoker and cold smoke for 2–6 hours, ensuring the chamber temperature remains under 30°C/85°F for the entire time the meat is in the smoker. The smoking time required will depend on your smoker, but generally the longer the process the richer the taste, with 2 hours for a lighter smoke and 6 hours for a stronger taste.

Once smoked, allow to cool, wrap in cling film (plastic wrap) and store in an airtight container in the refrigerator for up to 2 weeks.

For the best presentation, use a slicing machine and, for easier slicing, semi-freeze the belly beforehand so it is firm. You can slice the belly with a sharp knife if you do not have a slicing machine but the meat will need to be at refrigerator temperature.

For longer storage, cut the belly into 3–4 pieces and wrap with cling film then freeze. Defrost overnight in the refrigerator when required.

→ SMOKED BURGER PATTIES

THESE SMOKED MEAT PATTY RECIPES ARE VERY VERSATILE FOR EITHER GRILLING (BROILING), FRYING OR COOKING ON THE BARBECUE. SMOKING THE MEAT BEFORE MAKING IT INTO PATTIES GIVES YOUR BURGERS A BEAUTIFUL TASTE.

PORK PATTIES

Often beef is used in patties but I find pork a great meat to use because it is tasty, binds well and lends itself to a variety of complementary ingredients.

2¼ lb (1 kg) pork shoulder, cut into 1¼ in
  (3 cm) cubes
1½ tablespoons flaky sea salt
1 teaspoon sweet smoked paprika
¼ teaspoon ground black pepper
2 fl oz (¼ cup/60 ml) beer
3 tablespoons tomato sauce
1 teaspoon raw (demerara) sugar
¼ teaspoon ground fennel seeds
¼ teaspoon dried sage
oil, for frying

I like to use maple wood, fruit woods or a blend for these patties but use whatever you prefer. You will need enough wood or wood pellets for a 1-hour smoke.

Place all the ingredients in a large bowl and marinate in the refrigerator overnight.

Once the smoker is producing smoke, place the pork on a tray and put it into the smoker. Set your smoker to cold smoke and smoke for 1 hour, ensuring the chamber temperature remains under 30°C/85°F for the entire time the meat is in the smoker.

Remove and return the meat to the refrigerator for 30 minutes. Next, mince (grind) the pork on a medium plate, then mix the meat and the remaining ingredients together well, either by hand or with a paddle attachment on your food mixer. Form into patties.

To cook, heat a large frying pan over a medium heat and add a little oil. Fry the patties on one side for around 3-4 minutes then turn them over and fry for 3-4 minutes more, or until just cooked. Try to avoid pressing them down with your turning utensil as you want them to retain as much moisture as possible. Once cooked let the patties rest for a minute or two before serving.

LAMB PATTIES

Try to make sure the meat is not too fatty, as sometimes lamb can be. Don't let that put you off as these patties are very tasty.

2¼ lb (1 kg) lean lamb shoulder
1½ tablespoons flaky sea salt
1 teaspoon raw (demerara) sugar
½ teaspoon ground black pepper
1 tablespoon whole grain mustard
½ teaspoon dried rosemary
3 garlic cloves, crushed
8 fl oz (1 cup/250 ml) water

Follow the method for the pork patties. The wood blend I often use here is half maple and half hickory but use whatever you prefer.

VENISON PATTIES

Venison is a lean meat which is why pork fat has been added; if you are a hunter, this is a good recipe for using up any trim you have.

2 lb (900 g) venison meat
4½ oz (120 g) clean pork back fat
1½ tablespoons flaky sea salt
½ teaspoon ground black pepper
3 garlic cloves, crushed
¼ teaspoon dried thyme
3 tablespoons tomato sauce
2 tablespoons rice flour
4 fl oz (½ cup/125 ml) water

Follow the method for the pork patties. The wood blend I like to use here is half maple and half cherry wood but use whatever you prefer.

BEEF PATTIES

We are all familiar with beef patties but these are a good change from the usual. The smokiness adds a depth you don't get with standard beef patties.

2¼ lb (1 kg) beef chuck including fat cap, cut into 1¼ in (3 cm) cubes
1½ tablespoons flaky sea salt
½ teaspoon ground black pepper
1 teaspoon raw (demerara) sugar
3 tablespoons tomato sauce
2 garlic cloves, crushed
1 tablespoon paprika
2 fl oz (¼ cup/60 ml) beer
2 tablespoons rice flour
1 tablespoon Dijon mustard

Follow the method for the pork patties. The wood blend I like to use here is half hickory and half oak but use whatever you prefer.

PASTRAMI & SWISS CHEESE

Pastrami with bagels is a classic combination, and my first choice use for this cured meat. This is a quick and easy way to enjoy your own homemade pastrami.

4 fresh bagels
14 oz (400 g) sliced pastrami
  (see page 24)
butter, for spreading
chutney, for spreading
8 slices Swiss cheese
4 gherkins, sliced
4 vine-ripened tomatoes, sliced
salt and pepper, to taste

→ SERVES 4

Preheat the oven to 160°C/350°F/Gas mark 3. Line a baking tray with baking paper.

Slice the bagels in half and place under a hot grill (broiler) with the cut side up. Toast for 1–2 minutes until warmed through.

Meanwhile, arrange the pastrami in a single layer on the lined tray and place in the oven for 2–3 minutes to warm through.

Butter both sides of the bagels. Spread some chutney on the bottom half then top with the pastrami and gherkins, then the cheese. Return to the grill for 1 minute.

Remove from the grill, add the tomatoes and season with salt and pepper. Place the top half back on and enjoy!

SMOKED LAMB SHOULDER WITH ASPARAGUS & EGGPLANT SALAD

This recipe for lamb shoulder is a little more demanding to make but is well worth the time and effort. The tasty simple salad is great when the asparagus season begins and especially good cooked on the barbecue.

FOR THE ASPARAGUS & EGGPLANT SALAD

1 eggplant (aubergine), cut into ⅜ in (1 cm) thick discs
1 lb 2 oz (500 g) asparagus, trimmed
1 red onion, cut into wedges, keeping the core
2 red capsicums (bel peppers), de seeded and cut into ¾–1¼ in) 2–3 cm squares
3–4 tablespoons olive oil
3 tablespoons red wine vinegar
1 tablespoon balsamic vinegar
salt and pepper, to taste

1 smoked lamb shoulder (see page 29)

→ SERVES 6

Heat a grill (broiler) pan or the barbecue to a medium to high heat, and grill (broil) all the vegetables until tender. Cut the asparagus stems in half and place all the vegetables in a bowl. Season with the olive oil, vinegars and salt and pepper, and toss lightly.

Serve warm with sliced smoked lamb shoulder.

SMOKED CHICKEN SALAD

Smoked chicken is always popular and this salad is a great way to start a meal. Serve it as an entrée or in a large bowl at any summer barbecue.

1 iceberg lettuce, washed and shredded
1 lb 2 oz (500 g) smoked chicken (see page 28), shredded
1¾ oz (50 g) Parmesan, shaved
4 vine-ripened tomatoes, quartered
3½ oz (100 g) feta, diced
3½ oz (100 g) pickled red onions
3½ fl oz (100 ml) garlic dressing (see page 150)
salt and pepper, to taste
1 handful fresh croutons (see page 153)
1 tablespoon chopped Italian parsley

→ SERVES 6

Place the iceberg lettuce, chicken, Parmesan, tomatoes, feta, pickled onions and dressing in a large bowl. Season with salt and pepper and gently toss to mix together.

Place in serving bowls and garnish with the croutons and parsley.

SMOKED HAM & PEA SOUP

This soup is a real winter winner. Served with fresh crusty bread it's hard to beat as far as soups go. It will also freeze well, so save some for those nights when you want something quick and tasty to eat.

3 garlic cloves, crushed
2 onions, diced
1 large carrot, chopped
2 sticks celery, chopped
oil, for cooking
1 large smoked ham hock (see page 36)
7 oz (200 g) dried split peas
1 bay leaf
5¼ pints (3 litres) vegetable stock
7 oz (200 g) fresh or frozen peas
salt and pepper, to taste

➔ SERVES 4–6

Place the garlic, onions, carrots and celery in a food processor and pulse until finely diced.

Add a little oil to a large pan and heat on a medium to high heat. Add the onion mixture and sauté until soft before adding the hock, split peas, bay leaf and stock.

Bring to the boil and simmer until the split peas are cooked and the hock is falling from the bone, approximately 2–2½ hours. If the liquid falls below the hock, top up with water or add more stock.

Remove the hock and cool for 5 minutes, then remove the bone and chop the meat into ⅜ in (1 cm) pieces.

Return half the liquid and some of the split peas and vegetables to the food processor, add the fresh or frozen peas and purée together until smooth. Return to the pan and bring back to the boil. Add the meat and season with salt and pepper, if needed.

Serve with a chunk of crusty bread.

SMOKED BACON ARANCINI

I have always enjoyed making and eating mushroom risotto. This comes in a different form – crumbed and deep-fried risotto balls – but is equally as good. I often use these as finger food for functions and you could serve them as a taster before a meal.

FOR THE RISOTTO
¾ oz (20 g) butter
3½ oz (100 g) onion, diced
5 oz (150 g) smoked bacon (hot or cold, see pages 30 and 38), finely chopped
⅓ oz (10 g) dried forest mushrooms, soaked for 20 minutes, finely chopped
7 oz (200 g) fresh field (portobello) mushrooms, finely chopped
9 oz (250 g) arborio rice
3½ fl oz (100 ml) white wine
17 fl oz (500 ml) hot vegetable stock
½ teaspoon vegetable stock powder (optional)
1 oz (25 g) Parmesan, shaved
salt and pepper, to taste

TO ASSEMBLE
5 oz (150 g) plain (all-purpose) flour
1 egg
¼ pint (150 ml) milk
10½ oz (300 g) panko (or traditional) breadcrumbs)
vegetable oil, to deep-fry

➜ MAKES 18–24 PIECES

FOR THE RISOTTO

Add the butter to a large pan over a medium heat, then add the onions and sauté until transparent. Add the chopped bacon, soaked dried mushrooms and fresh mushrooms, and cook, continually stirring for 3–4 minutes, until the mushrooms are soft.

Add the rice and stir for another 1 minute, then add the white wine and cook until all the wine has been absorbed. If your vegetable stock is weak add the stock powder. Slowly add the stock a little at a time, stirring frequently, until the rice is *al dente* (just cooked). You may need more or less stock depending on how quickly the rice cooks. Once the rice is cooked remove from the heat, add the Parmesan and season with salt and pepper.

Transfer the risotto to a tray and spread it out to cool. Once cold, roll the risotto mix into balls about the size of a heaped tablespoon.

TO ASSEMBLE

Using 3 bowls of equal size, add the flour to 1 bowl, the beaten milk and egg to another, and the panko breadcrumbs to the last.

Place 4 balls at a time in the flour, coat lightly and then dip in the egg mix and coat in the breadcrumbs. You may like to re-crumb them in the egg and the breadcrumbs for a thicker crust.

Add 2 in (5 cm) of oil to a saucepan and heat to 175°C (350°F). Cook the risotto balls in batches until golden brown and hot in the middle.

Serve with lemon aïoli (see page 151) and a balsamic reduction (see page 152).

SMOKED VENISON WITH APPLE CHUTNEY & PORT WINE PUREE

This is a tasty starter for a dinner party or great as a light lunch. Making the chutney and port wine purée will take a little extra time but both will keep well in the refrigerator and can also be used with cheese boards or meat platters.

FOR THE PORT WINE PURÉE
1¾ fl oz (50 ml) water
1¾ oz (50 g) granulated (white) sugar
¼ pint (150 ml) port wine
8 fl oz (250 ml) red wine
6 g agar agar

→ MAKES 1 CUP

TO ASSEMBLE
14 oz (400 g) smoked venison loin (see page 28)
3½ oz (100 g) apple chutney (see page 151)

→ SERVES 4

FOR THE PURÉE

Place all the ingredients in a medium pan and bring to the boil. Simmer gently for 10 minutes until the agar agar has dissolved. Transfer to a bowl to cool, then place in the refrigerator to set.

Once set, place the mixture in a blender and purée on high speed until smooth.

Place in an airtight container and store in the refrigerator until required, or for up to 2–3 weeks.

TO ASSEMBLE

Thinly slice the venison and divide into 4 portions with about 8 slices per portion and set aside. Place alongside a spoonful of chutney and port wine purée.

CASSOULET OF SMOKED SAUSAGES

I have always enjoyed cassoulet on colder nights; it takes a little time to prepare but is well worth it. Try this with a smoked slow-cooked ham hock for a really hearty winter meal.

1 lb 2 oz (500 g) dried cannellini beans, soaked overnight in 5¼ pints (3 litres) water
1 large onion
3 garlic cloves
2 medium carrots
1 stick celery
¼ leek
1 tablespoon lard or duck fat
3½ oz (100 g) uncooked smoked bacon (see page 30), chopped including rind
3½ oz (100 g) smoked chorizo (see page 33), sliced
7 oz (200 g) smoked pork sausages (see page 33), sliced
1 x 14 oz (400 g) can crushed tomatoes
12 fl oz (375 ml) veal or chicken stock
1 sprig thyme
1 bay leaf
2 teaspoons sweet smoked paprika
2 tablespoons tomato paste
1 tablespoon red wine vinegar
salt and pepper, to taste
1 handful breadcrumbs
finely chopped parsley, to garnish

→ SERVES 6

Place the drained beans in a large saucepan and cover with water. Bring to the boil and cook for 20 minutes, then drain and set aside.

Preheat the oven to 160-170°C/325-340°F/Gas mark 3-3½.

Lightly chop the onion, garlic, carrot, celery and leek in a food processor.

Put the lard or duck fat into a large pan set over a medium heat. Sauté the vegetables, bacon and sausages together lightly. Place this mixture into a large ovenproof dish. Add the beans, tomatoes, stock, herbs, paprika, tomato paste and vinegar. Season with salt and pepper.

Bake uncovered in the oven for 3-4 hours, or until the beans are soft. Remove from the oven and stir the mixture lightly, then top with the breadcrumbs. Increase the oven temperature to 190-200°C/375-400°F/Gas mark 5-6 and bake for another 12-15 minutes, until golden brown.

To serve, garnish with finely chopped parsley.

SMOKED VEAL TONGUE WITH SHERRY VINAIGRETTE

Tongue is coming into fashion again and this recipe makes a really good starter. Alternatively, serve it as a sharing plate – you will be surprised at how popular it is.

1 smoked veal tongue
  (see page 36)
1 bay leaf
8 peppercorns
½ teaspoon salt

FOR THE SHERRY VINAIGRETTE
1 red onion, diced
5 tablespoons sherry vinegar
2 fl oz (60 ml) olive oil
3 tablespoons chopped parsley
3 tablespoons chopped capers
salt and pepper, to taste

SERVES 4–6

Place the tongue in a large pan and cover with cold water. Add the bay leaf, peppercorns and salt. Bring to the boil and simmer for 2½–3 hours, until tender. Use a small knife to pierce the tongue to check if it is cooked; the tongue should give no resistance.

Allow the meat to cool in the liquid. Once cool, peel the tongue to remove the tough outer layer of skin. Thinly slice the tongue lengthwise and arrange on a serving plate.

FOR THE SHERRY VINAIGRETTE
Combine the ingredients in a bowl, seasoning well with salt and pepper, and pour over the tongue. Serve immediately.

SMOKING FISH & SEAFOOD

TIPS AND TECHNIQUES FOR ALL THOSE WHO ARE ENTHUSIASTIC ABOUT FISHING AND WISH TO TRY NEW WAYS OF EATING THEIR CATCH.

HOT SMOKING FISH

SMOKING SEAFOOD IS A GREAT WAY TO HELP PRESERVE IT AND ALSO ADDS TASTE.

FAST METHOD

The fast method is best used for smaller fillets such as trout, snapper and salmon.

2¼ lb (1 kg) fish fillets
salt and pepper, to taste
brown sugar, to sprinkle
lemon zest, fresh herbs or spices

I like to use maple or apple wood for this type of smoking but you can use whatever you prefer. You will need enough wood or wood pellets for an 18-25-minute smoke.

Simply place your prepared fillets on a sheet of baking paper. Pat dry with a paper towel, lightly season with salt and pepper, then generously sprinkle brown sugar over the fish. You can also add any other ingredients such as lemon zest, spices such as sweet smoked paprika, or fresh herbs such as dill before smoking - enjoy experimenting.

Once your smoker is producing smoke, place the fish on a rack in the smoker and hot smoke for approximately 18-25 minutes, until the fish is just cooked through and has an internal temperature of around 60-65°C/140-150°F. When I say 'just cooked through' I mean that the flesh is still moist and not dry. Remove from the smoker and cool for a couple of minutes before eating.

For storage, wrap in cling film (plastic wrap) and store in an airtight container for 3-4 days.

SLOW METHOD

For the slow method the fillets are brined before smoking. This is a better method to use for larger fillets.

1¾ pints (1 litre) water
2 tablespoons salt
2 tablespoons sugar
lemon zest, fresh herbs or spices
4½ lb (2 kg) fish

I like to use an apple wood blend with tuna or marlin and apple or maple wood with salmon but use whatever you prefer. You will need enough wood or wood pellets for a 1-2-hour smoke.

Bring all the ingredients except for the fish to the boil in a large pan, then cool the solution to 4°C/39°F. Place the fish in the brine for between 2 and 36 hours, depending on the thickness and size of the fish. For example, I would leave a 2¼ lb (1 kg) salmon fillet for 12 hours, but a large 8¾ lb (4 kg) piece of marlin or tuna for 36 hours.

Once you have cured the fish for the desired length of time, wash under cold water and pat dry with paper towels then dry, uncovered, for 4-6 hours in the refrigerator.

Once your smoker is producing smoke, place the fish on a rack and put it in the smoker until the fish reaches an internal temperature of around 60-65°C/140-150°F. Cool for a couple of minutes and serve. For storage, wrap in cling film (plastic wrap) and store in an airtight container for up to 3-5 days.

HOT SMOKED FISH

(USING THE FAST METHOD, PAGE 60)

1. SEASON THE FISH WITH SALT AND BROWN SUGAR.

2. GET THE SMOKER READY WITH WOOD CHIPS.

4. PLACE THE FISH ON A RACK IN THE SMOKER.

5. COVER THE SMOKER WITH ALUMINIUM FOIL.

6. MAKE SURE THERE ARE NO GAPS FOR SMOKE TO ESCAPE.

3. HEAT THE SMOKER SO THAT IT STARTS PRODUCING SMOKE. TURN THE HEAT TO LOW AND ENSURE WOOD CHIPS BURN SLOWLY.

7. AFTER 15–20 MINUTES OPEN THE SMOKER AND CHECK THE FISH, BEING CAREFUL NOT TO LET IT DRY OUT.

8. THE FINISHED SMOKED FISH, READY TO SERVE.

HOT SMOKING SHELLFISH

MUSSELS, CLAMS AND OYSTERS CAN EITHER BE SMOKED RAW OR SOAKED IN BRINE FOR 20 MINUTES BEFORE SMOKING. I MAKE UP ENOUGH BRINE TO JUST COVER THE AMOUNT OF SHELLFISH I WANT TO SMOKE. DRAIN THE SHELLFISH FROM THE BRINE AND LET STAND FOR 5 MINUTES BEFORE SMOKING.

HOT SMOKED OYSTERS, MUSSELS & CLAMS

When hot smoking shellfish smoke them only until just opened. You want them to be smoked but not dried out and overcooked.

2¼ lb (1 kg) shellfish, such as mussels, clams and oysters

I like to use apple or cherry wood for smoking mussels or clams but use whatever you prefer. You will need enough wood or wood pellets for a 30-minute smoke.

Once your smoker is producing smoke, put the shellfish in a tray on a rack in the chamber and smoke until the shellfish begin to open. You want the shellfish to reach an internal temperature of 60°C/140°F. With a stove top smoker this process will usually take 15–20 minutes.

At this stage turn the heat off and let the shellfish stand for 5 minutes before removing them from the smoker. It is important to discard any shellfish that do not open.

SHELLFISH BRINE

1¾ pints (1 litre) water
2 tablespoons salt
2 tablespoons sugar
lemon zest, fresh herbs or spices

Bring all the brine ingredients to the boil, then cool the solution to 4°C/39°F. Place the shellfish just covered in the brine for approximately 20 minutes. Drain the brine and leave the shellfish to stand for 5 minutes before smoking.

COLD SMOKING SEAFOOD

COLD SMOKING SEAFOOD IS A GREAT WAY TO PRESERVE A FRESH CATCH. IT TAKES LONGER THAN HOT SMOKING BUT THE RESULTS ARE WELL WORTH THE EXTRA TIME.

COLD SMOKED OYSTERS

If you plan on making battered smoked oysters or any other recipe that requires raw oysters, cold smoking is the method to use.

1 dozen oysters in the half shell

I like to use the lighter woods such as apple or cherry for oysters but use whatever you prefer. You will need enough wood or wood pellets for a 30-minute smoke.

Once your smoker is producing smoke place the oysters in a tray on a rack in the smoker and cold smoke for up to 30 minutes. Ensure the chamber temperature remains under 20°C/68°F for the entire time the oysters are in the smoker. Use within 1 day.

COLD SMOKED SCALLOPS

Smoked scallops are great lightly sautéed in a very hot pan until they get a little browned. Finish with a dot of butter, and ensure they are not overcooked. I prefer them just warm on the inside.

12 large scallops out of the shell

As with the oysters, I like to use a lighter wood such as apple or cherry, but use whatever you prefer. You will need enough wood or wood pellets for a 30-minute smoke.

With a paper towel, pat the scallops dry and place them onto a fine mesh rack. Once the smoker is producing smoke place the scallops in the smoker and cold smoke for up to 30 minutes. Ensure the chamber does not exceed 20°C/68°F for the entire time the scallops are in the smoker. Use within 1 day.

COLD SMOKED SALMON

There are a number of ways you can prepare salmon for cold smoking. This 'dry' method is the one I always use as it helps draw out a lot of water in the curing process and the final product isn't too salty. To incorporate more complex tastes, try adding different ingredients into the salt and sugar mix before curing the fish. Alternatively, you can place the salmon to cure in a brine (see page 60) for 1–2 days, before drying and smoking. The following recipe can also be used for trout, or other oily fish.

3½ oz (100 g) salt
7 oz (200 g) sugar
lemon zest, fresh herbs or spices, or various
  peppers such as Szechuan pepper
2¼ lb (1 kg) side fresh salmon (deboned, skin
  on)

I like to use apple wood to cold smoke salmon, but use whatever you prefer. You will need enough wood or wood pellets for a 3-6-hour smoke.

Mix the salt and sugar, along with any other ingredients you are using, together in a small bowl.

Arrange a large sheet of aluminium foil on a clean work surface and evenly spread half the salt and sugar mix on it, roughly in the shape of the fillet. Place the salmon fillet, skin side down on the salt and sugar and top evenly with the remaining mix. Wrap up tightly and place in a deep-sided tray. Store the wrapped fish in the refrigerator for up to 48 hours, turning the salmon after 24 hours. For smaller fillets of around 1 lb 9 oz–2¼ lb (700 g–1 kg) cure the fish in the salt and sugar mix for 36 hours. If the fillets weigh between 2¼ and 3 lb 6 oz (1 and 1.5 kg), leave them for up to 72 hours.

After the desired time, remove the fillet from the foil and wash off any salt mix under cold running water. Pat dry with paper towels and leave overnight, uncovered, in the refrigerator to dry.

Once the smoker is producing smoke, place the cured salmon fillet on a rack in the smoking chamber and cold smoke for 3-6 hours, depending on how much smoke you want. Make sure the chamber temperature remains under 20°C/68°F for the entire time the fish is in the smoker.

Once smoked it's ready to eat, although it will mellow if you leave it uncovered overnight in the refrigerator.

For storage, wrap in cling film (plastic wrap) and store in an airtight container in the refrigerator for up to 8 days, or freeze.

→ COLD SMOKED SALMON

1. FRESH SALMON WITH BONES REMOVED AND SKIN ON THE FILLET.

2. SPRINKLE HALF OF THE SALT AND SUGAR CURING MIX OVER A LARGE PIECE OF ALUMINIUM FOIL.

6. TRANSFER THE SALMON PARCEL TO CURE IN THE REFRIGERATOR FOR UP TO 48 HOURS, TURNING AFTER 24 HOURS.

7. UNWRAP AND WASH OFF THE CURING MIX . DRY OVERNIGHT IN THE REFRIGERATOR, UNCOVERED.

3. ARRANGE THE SALMON FILLET ONTO THE CURING MIX.

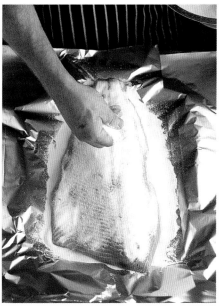

4. COVER THE FILLET WITH THE REMAINING CURING MIX.

5. WRAP THE SALMON IN THE ALUMINIUM FOIL.

8. THE CURED SALMON READY TO BE SMOKED.

9. THE CURED SALMON BEING SMOKED.

10. THE FINISHED COLD SMOKED SALMON.

SMOKED SALMON FISH CAKES WITH SALSA

These fish cakes make an easy and tasty starter. I like to serve them with poached eggs and hollandaise for brunch – an enjoyable breakfast!

1 lb 2 oz (500 g) smoked, deboned and skinned salmon

FOR THE FISH CAKES
14 oz (400 g) potatoes, peeled and chopped
½ teaspoon salt
2 tablespoons crème fraîche
½ teaspoon sweet smoked paprika
½ teaspoon lemon zest
1 egg
1 tablespoon chopped parsley
1 spring onion (scallion), finely sliced
salt and pepper, to taste
oil, for frying

FOR THE SALSA
3 large tomatoes, deseeded and diced
½ small red onion, finely diced
1 tablespoon red wine vinegar
2 tablespoons olive oil
2 tablespoons chopped coriander (cilantro)
salt and pepper, to taste

→ **MAKES 10–12 CAKES**

FOR THE FISH

You can use either the fast or slow method of smoking (see page 60). I like to use a half and half blend of wood for the smoke. You will need enough wood or wood pellets for a 45-minute to 1-hour smoke or until the fish reaches an internal temperature of 60°C/140°F.

FOR THE FISH CAKES

Place the potatoes in a medium pan, cover with water, add the salt and bring to the boil. Cook until soft. Use a small knife to pierce a potato: if cooked the potato should give no resistance.

Drain well, place into a large bowl and crush the potatoes well with a fork. Then add the remaining ingredients, including the fish, season well with salt and pepper, and gently mix together.

Form the mixture into 10-12 cakes weighing roughly 3 oz (70-80 g) each. Refrigerate to firm for 30 minutes.

Add a little oil to a large frying pan over a medium heat, then fry the smoked fish cakes until golden brown on each side.

FOR THE SALSA

Place all ingredients into a bowl and mix lightly, seasoning well with salt and pepper. Serve at room temperature.

Serve the fish cakes warm with salsa or enjoy with poached eggs for breakfast.

SMOKED MUSSEL FRITTERS WITH CAPER MAYONNAISE

Fritters are one of the best ways to enjoy mussels and these are tasty and simple to put together. If you don't want to use smoked mussels, just very lightly cook the fresh mussels. These are great as smaller fritters for a snack or canapé. Smoked snapper can be substituted for the mussels too. Serve hot with caper mayonnaise (see page 150).

2 eggs
8 fl oz (250 ml) milk
8 oz (225 g) self-raising
  (self-rising) flour
10½ oz (300 g) hot smoked
  mussels, diced or (2¼ lb/
  1 kg) raw weight with shells)
3 garlic cloves (roasted, if
  preferred)
1 tablespoon chopped parsley
3 oz (85 g/½ cup) freshly cooked
  or defrosted frozen sweetcorn
  kernels
1 spring onion (scallion), finely
  sliced
½ red chilli, de seeded and diced
vegetable oil, for cooking

➔ MAKES 14–18 FRITTERS

In a bowl beat the eggs, milk and flour together to form a thick batter. Add the remaining ingredients except for the vegetable oil.

Add a little oil to a large frying pan over a medium heat and fry large spoonfuls of the mixture until golden brown on one side, then turn and brown on the other.

VARIATION

To cook fresh unsmoked mussels, heat a large pan with a lid to very hot. Add the mussels and 2 fl oz (¼ cup/60 ml) white wine, cover and shake the pan over the heat while holding the lid on. Cook until the first mussels start to open then transfer them as they open into a large high-sided tray and allow to cool. Remove from the shells when cool enough to handle and dice. Follow the method above.

Discard any mussels that are open before cooking and any that fail to open after cooking.

BATTERED SMOKED OYSTERS

Deep-fried oysters are fantastic to eat (as are most deep-fried foods!) and make a great starter or canapé. This batter also works well with fish, and I often use it for my fish and chips at home after a successful day on the water.

24 cold smoked oysters

FOR THE BATTER

11 fl oz (330 ml) lager beer
1–2 oz (30–60 g/¼–½ cup) self-raising (self-rising) flour, plus extra for coating
salt and pepper, to taste
oil, for deep-frying

→ SERVES 2–4

Remove the oysters from their shells and place on paper towels.

FOR THE BATTER

Pour the beer into a bowl and while whisking slowly, add enough flour to form a smooth batter. Season with salt and pepper and set aside.

Add 2 in (5 cm) of oil to a pan and heat to 175°C/350°F.

Lightly coat each oyster in flour then dip in the batter and fry in the oil until golden brown.

Cook only 6-8 oysters at a time to retain the temperature of the oil and so that the oysters cook consistently.

Serve hot with a little caper mayonnaise (see page 150) or your choice of dipping sauce.

HOT SMOKED OYSTERS KILPATRICK

These oysters make a great snack - a smoked version of a classic dish - or serve them as a canapé or starter at a dinner party. They are easily made ahead of time and smoked when needed.

1 tablespoon butter
1 onion, diced
5 slices smoked bacon (see page 38), diced
2 tablespoons Worcestershire sauce
2 tablespoons lemon juice
1 tablespoon chopped parsley
salt and pepper, to taste
24 Pacific oysters, in the half shell

→ SERVES 2–4

I like to use maple wood with these oysters but use whatever you prefer. You will need enough wood or wood pellets for a 15-20-minute smoke.

Melt the butter in a frying pan over a medium heat, add the onion and cook until transparent. Add the bacon and cook for another 2-3 minutes, then remove from the heat and mix in the Worcestershire sauce, lemon juice and chopped parsley. Season lightly with salt and pepper.

Place the oysters on a tray and spoon the mixture evenly over the top.

Once the smoker is producing smoke, place the oysters in the smoker until warmed through, around 15-20 minutes, and they reach an internal temperature of 60°C/140°F. Serve hot.

HOT SMOKED SALMON, POTATO BLINI & PICKLED RED ONIONS

Freshly smoked salmon served with these light blini makes a wonderful dish.

FOR THE PICKLED ONIONS
1 lb 2 oz (500 g) red onions
3½ fl oz (100 ml) white wine vinegar
4½ oz (125 g) caster (superfine) sugar
1 cinnamon quill (stick)
3 whole cloves
1 chilli, cut lengthways
¾ teaspoon salt

→ MAKES 2½ CUPS

FOR THE POTATO BLINI
1 lb 6 oz (600 g) potatoes, peeled
3 tablespoons milk
3 tablespoons plain (all-purpose) flour
3 egg yolks
3 tablespoons crème fraîche
3 egg whites, whisked to soft peaks
salt and white pepper, to taste
oil, for cooking

14 oz (400 g) hot smoked salmon (see page 60), flaked

→ SERVES 4–6

FOR THE PICKLED ONIONS

Peel, wash and slice the red onions. Allow to dry well.

Place the remaining ingredients in a large pan over a high heat and bring to the boil, then add the onions. Turn the heat down to medium and cook until the onions are tender, approximately 5-7 minutes.

Set aside to cool. Once cool, place in an airtight container in the refrigerator for up to 2 weeks. Remove the cinnamon, cloves and chilli before serving.

FOR THE POTATO BLINI

Place the potatoes in a large pan, cover with water then bring to the boil. Cook until soft, the tip of a knife should meet no resistance when pierced into a potato. Drain and allow to dry for 2-3 minutes, then pass through a ricer or mouli. The mixture should be dry.

Beat in the milk then the flour. Add the egg yolks one at a time, mixing well with each addition, then add the crème fraîche and fold in the whisked egg whites. Season with salt and white pepper.

For best results, cook spoonfuls with a very small amount of oil on the flat plate of a sandwich press or gently cook in a non-stick frying pan until golden brown on both sides.

Serve warm topped with pickled red onion and some flaked hot smoked salmon.

COLD SMOKED SALMON WITH PUMPERNICKEL

Cold smoked salmon is my best-loved cold smoked fish and serving it with pumpernickel is an age-old tradition. I have added crème fraîche and cream cheese to enhance the dish, as some people find pumpernickel a little dry.

3½ oz (100 g) cream cheese
salt and pepper, to taste
10½ oz (300 g) pumpernickel
   (rye) bread, sliced
3½ oz (100 g) crème fraîche
1 teaspoon chopped chives

TO ASSEMBLE
14 oz (400 g) cold smoked
   salmon (see page 66), sliced
rocket (arugula) leaves to
   garnish
2 teaspoons capers
olive oil, to drizzle

→ SERVES 4

Place the cream cheese in a small bowl and season with salt and pepper. Mix well.

Spread the slices of pumpernickel with the cream cheese, leaving 1 slice plain for the top layer. Spread the cream cheese right to the edges.

To layer, place 1 slice on top of the next with the cream cheese facing upward then top with the plain slice. This will form a layered loaf. Wrap the layered loaf with cling film (plastic wrap) and place in the refrigerator for 20 minutes before slicing.

Add the crème fraîche, chives and salt and pepper to taste to another bowl, and mix well.

TO ASSEMBLE
To serve, arrange the salmon on a plate, add 1 slice of pumpernickel and a spoonful of crème fraîche. Garnish with the rocket leaves, capers and olive oil.

JOHN'S SMOKED TUNA SALAD

This salad is my take on my stepfather's recipe. He uses canned tuna whereas I use hot smoked tuna fillets. We often have this in the refrigerator to have on our sandwiches at lunchtime. This is also a lovely simple salad to enjoy with any summer barbecue.

10½ oz (300 g) hot smoked tuna
7 oz (200 g) cabbage, thinly sliced
5 oz (150 g) carrot, grated (shredded)
2 small red onions, finely sliced
2–3 shakes Tabasco sauce
1 tablespoon brown sauce
3 tablespoons thousand island dressing
1 tablespoon Worcestershire sauce
3 tablespoons olive oil
1 tablespoon chopped parsley
4 tablespoons mayonnaise
2 tablespoons balsamic vinegar
salt and pepper, to taste

→ SERVES 4

FOR THE TUNA

You can use either the fast or slow method for smoking the tuna (see page 60). I like to use a half-and-half blend of wood for the smoke, but use whatever you prefer. You will need enough wood or wood pellets for a 1–1½-hour smoke, or until the internal temperature reaches 60°C/140°F.

Place the tuna in a large bowl and lightly break up the fish with a fork.

Add the remaining ingredients and gently mix together until well incorporated.

SMOKED SNAPPER PIE

When I had my restaurant, I'd occasionally smoke some of my weekend catch for pies for staff; it was my way of letting my staff enjoy my fishing success. A young chef working for me at the time, made the best smoked fish pie. Here is my take on his version.

1 lb 2 oz (500 g) hot smoked snapper, bones and skin removed

FOR THE TOPPING
1 lb 2 oz (500 g) potatoes, peeled and chopped
½ teaspoon salt
1 oz (30 g) butter
2 fl oz (¼ cup/60 ml) milk (or half milk, half cream)
salt and pepper, to taste

FOR THE FILLING
17 fl oz (2 cups/500 ml) milk
3 tablespoons smoked butter (see page 89)
4 tablespoons plain (all-purpose) flour
1 small red onion, diced
4 oz (1 cup/115 g) frozen peas
6 oz (1 cup/175 g) sweetcorn kernels
1 teaspoon sweet smoked paprika
2 tablespoons chopped parsley
salt and pepper, to taste
3 hard-boiled eggs, peeled and quartered
2 oz (60 g) cheese, grated (shredded)

→ SERVES 6

You can use either the fast or slow method for smoking the snapper (see page 60). I like to use a half-and-half blend of wood for the smoke. You will need enough wood or wood pellets for a 30-45-minute smoke or until the fillets reach an internal temperature of 60°C/140°F.

FOR THE TOPPING
Place the potatoes in a pan, cover with cold water and add the salt. Bring to the boil and then simmer until the potatoes are cooked through. Use a small knife to pierce a potato: when cooked, the potato should give no resistance. Drain and return the potatoes in the pan to the stove top to dry over a low heat. Pass the hot dry potatoes through a mouli or potato ricer.

Heat the milk and butter then slowly add this mixture to the potatoes while stirring. The topping should be soft and smooth. Season well with salt and pepper.

FOR THE FILLING
Preheat the oven to 170°C/340°F/Gas mark 3½.

Heat the milk in a medium pan then remove the pan from the heat.

Melt the butter in a large pan then add the flour and cook for 2 minutes, stirring continuously. Slowly add the hot milk while continuing to stir, until combined. Continue cooking over a low heat, stirring continuously, for 10 minutes until thickened.

Add the onion, peas and sweetcorn and cook for 2-3 minutes. Remove from the heat and add the snapper, paprika and parsley, and season well.

Place the filling into a suitable-baking dish then add the egg quarters, pushing them into the filling a little. Top the filling with the mashed potato and sprinkle over the grated cheese.

Bake for 20-25 minutes until piping hot. Serve hot.

SMOKING DAIRY PRODUCTS, EGGS & NUTS

SOME RATHER MORE UNUSUAL AND TASTY VARIATIONS ON THE THEME.

SMOKING DAIRY PRODUCTS

Dairy foods must only be cold smoked to keep the integrity of the ingredient – you don't want butter to melt or cheese to get warm and become too soft. So the temperature of your smoker is very important and plays a big part in getting the best results.

In some of the recipes you'll only need a small amount of the smoked dairy product, otherwise the final dish can become too smoky. Smoked butter or cream will usually be blended together with an unsmoked amount of the same product before being served. The best way for you to understand why is to taste some unblended smoked butter – you will find that smoked butter on its own has a very strong taste and is really too bitter to eat as is.

Dairy foods do not need curing or brining, and can be placed straight in the smoker. If you are smoking a soft cheese, for instance mozzarella, it is a good idea to leave it uncovered overnight in the refrigerator before smoking. This allows the cheese to form a skin and helps with the browning.

Cream, butter, ricotta and quark can be put into a stainless steel tray and placed in the smoker for a cold smoke; firm cheeses can go straight on a rack or in a tray. How strong you would like the final taste will determine the time the food remains in the smoker. Bear in mind how you intend to use each smoked ingredient and be careful not to overpower the final dish.

Other cheeses suitable for smoking are Cheddar, Camembert, Edam, Brie, mozzarella and blue cheeses. The fuels I like to use are the sweeter fruit tree woods, such as apple and cherry, along with maple.

SMOKED CHOCOLATE

When smoking chocolate it is best to taste and assess the smokiness. If you use a fuel with a strong taste you might need to use part smoked chocolate and part unsmoked chocolate – you want a subtle smokiness in the end product, not an overpowering result.

1 lb 2 oz (500 g) dark (bittersweet), milk or white chocolate pieces

I like cherry wood with chocolate but use whatever you prefer. You will need enough wood or wood pellets for a 1-hour smoke.

Once the smoker is producing smoke, place the chocolate inside a deep dish or tray and place it on a rack in the smoker. Smoke for 1 hour, ensuring the chamber temperature remains under 20°C/68°F the entire time.

Remove the chocolate and store in the pantry in an airtight container for up to 1 month.

SMOKED BUTTER

If you like this butter it would be a good idea to make a large amount and store it in the freezer, taking out what you need for a few days at a time. Smoked butter has many uses, from finishing a steak, adding to mashed potatoes or serving with cooked beans. It is very versatile and great to have on hand.

**1 lb 2 oz (500 g) unsalted butter
salt**

I like cherry wood for butter but use whatever you prefer. You will need enough wood or wood pellets for a 2-hour smoke.

Cut the butter in half and place one half in a bowl and set aside.

Cut the other half into 2 pieces to provide more surface area for smoking. Once the smoker is producing smoke, place the butter inside a deep dish or tray and place it on a rack in the smoker. Cold smoke for 2 hours, ensuring the chamber temperature remains under 20°C/68°F the entire time. It is fine for the butter to soften but not to melt.

Lightly whip the smoked butter and the remaining unsmoked butter together with a small electric mixer and season well with the salt.

Take a large piece of baking paper and place the softened butter onto the paper and form into a roll. Chill in the refrigerator and slice when needed, or store in the freezer for a few months.

SMOKED CHEESE

Smoking cheese is an easy way to add smoky taste to a dish; you just have to be careful that the cheese doesn't get hot during the process or it will end up a melted mess.

1 lb 2 oz (500 g) cheese (Brie, Cheddar, blue cheese or mozzarella)

I like to use apple wood but use whatever you prefer. You will need enough wood or wood pellets for a 1-1½-hour smoke.

Once your smoker is producing smoke, place the cheese on a rack in the smoker and smoke for 1-1½ hours. The temperature in the chamber must remain under 20°C/68°F the entire time.

Remove the cheese from the smoker, wrap in baking paper and store in the refrigerator until ready to use.

SMOKED QUARK OR CREAM

I like smoking these types of dairy products to give taste to a final dish.

1 lb 2 oz (500 g) quark or cream

I like to use maple or fruit woods but use the wood you prefer. You will need enough for a 1-hour smoke.

Once your smoker is producing smoke, place the quark or cream in a deep dish or tray on a rack in the smoker and smoke for 1 hour. Make sure the chamber temperature remains less than 30ºC/85ºF for the entire time.

Remove the dish of quark or cream from the smoker, cover with cling film (plastic wrap) and store in the refrigerator.

SMOKED MASCARPONE

2¼ lb (1 kg) smoked cream
2 tablespoons red wine vinegar
muslin cloth
string
small hook

In a large heavy pan heat the smoked cream until it comes to a boil then, using a large metal spoon, stir in the red wine vinegar. The cream should look split on the back of the spoon. Add a spoonful more vinegar if the cream doesn't look split. Once split, remove from the heat and allow to stand for 30 minutes.

Line a large bowl with muslin cloth and gently pour in the cream.

Place in the refrigerator overnight or until firm. The next day, bring the top of the cloth together and tie with string. Lift the wrapped cheese about 4 in (10 cm) above the bowl and hang over the bowl from a hook attached to a shelf in the refrigerator. Leave to hang overnight. After 24 hours remove the cheese from the cloth and store it in an airtight container in the refrigerator for up to 5 days

SMOKING EGGS

EGGS CAN BE SMOKED EITHER RAW OR HARD-BOILED DEPENDING ON THEIR FINAL USE. HARD-BOILED EGGS CAN BE SMOKED EITHER WITH OR WITHOUT THE SHELL. BY LEAVING THE SHELL ON YOU CAN ACHIEVE A SMOKED TASTE WITHOUT THE DARK TINTS YOU GET WHEN SMOKING SHELLED EGGS.

SMOKED RAW EGGS

I like to cold-smoke raw eggs for 3-4 hours.

As many eggs as you wish to smoke or your smoker will allow

I like hickory or cherry wood with raw eggs but use whatever you prefer. You will need enough wood or wood pellets for a 3-4 hour smoke.

Once the smoker is producing smoke, place the eggs on a rack in the smoker. Smoke for 3-4 hours, ensuring the chamber temperature remains less than 20°C/68°F the entire time.

Remove the eggs and place in a plastic bag or covered plastic container overnight before using. This helps them retain the smoke. For storage, keep for up to 1 week in the refrigerator.

SMOKED HARD-BOILED EGGS

If you want a deep finished tone to the eggs, peel them before smoking; if you want them to look like standard eggs, then smoke them in the shell. Smoked hard-boiled eggs are a great addition to salads such as the smoked egg and lamb's lettuce salad (see page 102), in sandwiches and in dishes such as the smoked snapper pie (see page 84).

12 hard-boiled eggs

I like hickory or cherry wood with hard-boiled eggs but use whatever you prefer. You will need enough wood or wood pellets for a 2-3-hour smoke in the shell, or a 30-45-minute smoke if the eggs are peeled.

Once the smoker is producing smoke, place the eggs on a rack in the smoker. Smoke for 2-3 hours for eggs in the shell ensuring the chamber temperature remains less than 30°C/85°F the entire time. For peeled eggs smoke for 30-45 minutes ensuring the temperature remains under 60°C/140°F.

Remove the eggs and use within 2 days.

SMOKING NUTS

NUTS ARE BEST COLD-SMOKED AND PRETTY MUCH ANY NUT CAN BE SMOKED. NUTS MAKE A GREAT SNACK WHEN SMOKED.

There are a number of different ways to finish smoked nuts. For instance, they can be roasted and tossed in your choice of seasoning while still hot from the oven, or smoked and then salted, which is essentially eating them raw.

You might find that the nuts will fall through the rungs on some smoking racks so either place them on a fine cake rack, baking tray or aluminium foil with a few holes poked in the foil to help the smoke filter through to the nuts.

SMOKED NUTS

2 tablespoons salt
24 fl oz (3 cups/750 ml) water
12 oz (3 cups/350 g) whole nuts (almonds,
  cashews or peanuts or any other nut)

I like to use a cherry or apple wood for nuts but use whatever you prefer. You will need enough wood or wood pellets for a 30-minute to 4-hour smoke.

Make a solution by dissolving the salt in the water. Add the nuts and soak for 10 minutes then drain the nuts and allow them to dry on the bench for around 1 hour. Once they have dried prepare the cold smoker.

Once the smoker is producing smoke, place the nuts onto a fine cake rack or a sheet of aluminium foil pierced with holes. Place the rack or foil in the smoker and allow the nuts to smoke for 30 mintues to 4 hours depending on the strength you require - 30 minutes will give a light smoky note and after 4 hours they will be very strong in taste.

Remove the nuts from the smoker.

At this stage you can either lightly salt the nuts, store them in an airtight container or preheat the oven to 170°C/340°F/Gas mark 3½ and roast the nuts for 10-15 minutes until lightly browned, making sure you stir them 2–3 times during cooking. Then lightly season with salt and cool. Store the nuts in an airtight container for up to 4 weeks.

# SMOKING SEEDS

SMOKED SEEDS CAN BE EATEN AS A SNACK LIKE NUTS OR ADDED TO BREADS OR SALADS TO ADD TASTE AND TEXTURE, AND TO MAKE THEM MORE INTERESTING. SEEDS ARE BEST SOAKED IN BRINE AS THIS WILL HELP WITH THE FINAL TASTE.

SMOKED SEEDS

2 tablespoons salt
24 fl oz (3 cups/750 ml) water
1 lb 2 oz (500 g) seeds (pumpkin or sunflower seeds)

I like to use maple or hickory wood but use whatever you prefer. You will need enough wood or wood pellets for a 2-3-hour smoke.

Dissolve the salt in the water, add the seeds and leave them to soak for 8 hours. Drain well and dry on the work top for 4-6 hours. Once they have dried prepare the cold smoker.

Once the smoker is producing smoke, place the seeds onto a fine cake rack or a sheet of aluminium foil pierced with holes. Place the rack or foil in the smoker and allow the seeds to smoke for 2-3 hours.

Remove the seeds.

At this stage you can either lightly salt the seeds, store them in an airtight container or dry roast them in a pan over a medium heat until lightly browned, making sure you stir them often during cooking. Or, if you prefer, roast them in the oven at 170°C/340°F/ Gas mark 3½ for 10-15 minutes. Then lightly season with salt and cool. Store the seeds in an airtight container for up to 2 months.

SMOKED SWEET & SPICY ALMONDS

If you like to try different varieties of nuts you could use hazelnuts, pecans, cashews or peanuts in this recipe, but I find almonds work particularly well. I enjoy them as a snack with some home-brewed beer.

½ teaspoon chilli powder
1½ teaspoons flaky sea salt
½ teaspoon garlic powder
1 teaspoon ground paprika
2 teaspoons melted butter
2 teaspoons liquid honey
1 lb 2 oz (500 g) cold smoked
  almonds (see page 94)

→ MAKES 3 CUPS

Preheat the oven to 170°C/340°F/Gas mark 3½. Line a baking tray with baking paper.

Combine the chilli powder, sea salt, garlic powder, paprika, melted butter and honey. Mix in the almonds, coating them well. Place on the prepared baking tray and roast for 12–18 minutes, stirring 2–3 times during the cooking process.

Allow to cool then store in an airtight container for up to 4 weeks.

SPRING LEAF SALAD WITH SMOKED SEEDS

This tasty and simple salad is quick and easy to make and lends itself to any outdoor event. The seeds bring the lettuce to life and add a little extra texture and bite. This salad goes well with a roast lamb leg or shoulder.

FOR THE VINAIGRETTE
1 tablespoon wholegrain mustard
½ teaspoon sugar
½ teaspoon salt
1½ fl oz (40 ml) red wine vinegar
¼ pint (150 ml) grapeseed oil

→ MAKES 175 ML

TO ASSEMBLE
9 oz (250 g) spring lettuce leaves
   (rocket/arugula, lollo bionda,
   lollo rosso, lamb's lettuce)
1½ oz (40 g) mixed smoked
   seeds (pumpkin and sunflower
   seeds, see page 95)
⅓ oz (10 g) mixed poppy seeds
   and sesame seeds
pinch of salt

→ SERVES 4–6

FOR THE VINAIGRETTE

Place the mustard, sugar, salt and vinegar into a bowl and whisk together While whisking continuously slowly drizzle in the grapeseed oil until incorporated.

Store in an airtight container in the refrigerator for up to 2 weeks.

TO ASSEMBLE

Carefully wash and dry the lettuce leaves taking care not to crush them. Add the leaves and seeds to a large serving bowl. Then gently mix in the vinaigrette and salt. Serve immediately.

SMOKED EGG & CHEESE OMELETTE

A simple breakfast or light meal, using smoked eggs brings a new dimension to the omelette. You can easily replace or add ingredients to make it your own.

vegetable oil, for cooking
3 smoked raw eggs
  (see page 92)
1 generous tablespoon single
  (light) cream
salt and pepper, to taste
1 oz (30 g) feta, diced
1 small vine-ripened tomato,
  sliced
2 basil leaves, ripped

→ SERVES 1

Heat a little oil in an omelette pan over a moderate heat.

Meanwhile, mix the eggs and the cream together, and season with salt and pepper. Ensure the pan is hot then pour the egg mixture into the pan. Using a fork, continuously drag the cooked egg from the outside into the centre. Once half the egg looks cooked, add the feta, sliced tomato and basil. Finish cooking the omelette on the stove until the egg is just cooked through, then remove it from the heat, gently fold and serve hot.

SMOKED EGG & LAMB'S LETTUCE SALAD

This is a classic salad we used to make when I worked in Lucerne in Switzerland. Called Nüsslisalat in Swiss German, this simple salad is very tasty with the smoked egg. You can serve it as an individual entrée salad or in a large bowl on the table to share along with some smoked lamb ribs (see page 34).

FOR THE VINAIGRETTE
1 tablespoon wholegrain mustard
½ teaspoon sugar
½ teaspoon salt
1½ fl oz (40 ml) red wine vinegar
¼ pint (150 ml) grapeseed oil

→ **MAKES 6 FL OZ (175 ML)**

9 oz (250 g) lamb's lettuce
2 smoked hard-boiled eggs,
  finely chopped
1 small red onion, finely chopped
3 fl oz (80 ml) vinaigrette
salt and pepper, to taste

→ **SERVES 4–6**

FOR THE VINAIGRETTE

Tip the mustard, sugar, salt and vinegar into a bowl and whisk together.

While whisking continuously, slowly drizzle in the grapeseed oil until incorporated.

Store in an airtight container in the refrigerator for up to 2 weeks.

TO ASSEMBLE

Carefully wash the lamb's lettuce, making sure to remove any roots and earth around the base of the stems, then dry gently. Place into a serving bowl with the base of the leaves all facing down, as if they were still growing in the ground.

Sprinkle over the chopped egg and red onion, dress with the vinaigrette and lightly season with salt and pepper. Serve at once.

BEER-CRUST BREAD WITH SMOKED BUTTER

Smoked butter adds a different dimension when spread on freshly baked crusty bread.

FOR THE BREAD DOUGH
13 fl oz (375 ml) tepid water
1 teaspoon active dried yeast
1 lb 6 oz (600 g) strong white
   bread flour, plus extra for
   dusting
1½ tablespoons salt

FOR THE TOPPING
3¾ fl oz (110 ml) beer
¼ teaspoon active dried yeast
3 oz (80 g) wholemeal
   (wholewheat) flour

smoked butter (see page 89) to
   serve

→ **MAKES 10 ROLLS**

FOR THE BREAD DOUGH

Mix the water and yeast together in a large bowl, then add the flour and salt and combine to form a dough. Knead the dough for 5-7 minutes by hand to develop the gluten in the flour.

Place in a clean bowl, cover with cling film (plastic wrap) and leave in a warm draught-free place to prove and double in size, several hours.

Turn out onto a clean work surface lightly dusted with flour and divide the dough into 10 portions. Roll each portion into an oval roll and place on a baking tray lined with baking paper and lightly dusted with flour. Return the tray to the warm draught-free place and leave to stand for 10 minutes.

FOR THE TOPPING

Place the beer and yeast together in a bowl and mix in the flour to form a batter. Let stand for 10 minutes then brush this onto the rolls and leave them to double in size.

Preheat the oven to 200°C/400°F/Gas mark 6 and place a small ovenproof bowl filled with about 8 fl oz (1 cup/250 ml) of water in the base of the oven. This will help the bread to rise during baking.

Once the rolls have doubled in size, lightly dust them with flour and place in the oven. After 10 minutes, reduce oven temperature down to 180°C/350°F/Gas mark 4 and bake for another 5-7 minutes, or until dark brown.

Allow to cool and serve warm with the smoked butter.

COURGETTE FLOWERS WITH SMOKED QUARK

This beautiful fresh and tasty dish is a good way of using up courgette flowers if you grow your own vegetables. You can also find courgette flowers at local markets when in season. If you can find female flowers with the small courgette still attached, all the better.

10½ oz (300 g) smoked quark (see page 90)
7 oz (200 g) ricotta
2 tablespoons chopped parsley
2 tablespoons finely sliced chives
2 tablespoons chopped basil
3 tablespoons Parmesan
salt and pepper, to taste
batter mix (see page 74)
oil, for frying
8 courgette (zucchini) flowers
flour, for dusting
fresh herbs, for garnish
4 tablespoons liquid honey

→ SERVES 4

Place 3½ oz (100 g) of the smoked quark with the ricotta, parsley, chives, basil and Parmesan in a large bowl and mix together well. Season with salt and pepper.

Make the batter following the method for the oysters on page 74.

Heat 2 in (5 cm) of oil in a large frying pan over a medium heat to 175°C/350°F.

Fill each flower with the quark and ricotta mixture. Lightly coat each flower in flour, then dip into the batter mix and gently place in the hot oil.

Cook, using a slotted spoon to turn the flowers when golden brown on one side. When golden brown on both sides carefully remove and drain on paper towels. Repeat until all the flowers are cooked.

Serve with the remaining smoked quark and fresh herbs and drizzle over the honey.

GRILLED CHICKEN WITH SMOKED BRIE & BASIL

This quick and easy dish is a great summer meal. Try serving it with the smoked tomato chutney (see page 126) and a simple rocket (arugula) salad.

4 skinless chicken breasts
oil, for cooking
salt and pepper, to taste
16 large basil leaves
16 sun-dried tomatoes
1 x 4½ oz (125 g) smoked Brie
  (see page 89), sliced

→ **SERVES 4**

Preheat the grill (broiler) to 220°C/425°F/Gas mark 7. Line a baking tray with baking paper.

On a chopping board place 1 chicken breast skin side up, and with a sharp knife slice the breast in half horizontally by holding the knife parallel to the board and cutting through. Repeat with the remaining chicken breasts until you have 8 thin slices.

Lightly brush the chicken pieces with oil and season with salt and pepper. Heat a griddle pan on a medium heat and grill (broil) the chicken until just cooked through.

Place the chicken pieces on the prepared tray. Place two basil leaves and two sun-dried tomatoes on each piece of chicken. Season with pepper and top with a slice of Brie. Place the chicken under the grill to melt the cheese. Serve warm.

SMOKED POTATO GRATIN

This recipe is one of my preferred ways to eat potatoes. When I was a guest chef on a cruise ship I served this recipe with roast eye fillet (tenderloin), though it goes equally well with roast lamb or chicken. It does need to be made in advance if you cut it into portions as in this recipe, but if you are short on time serve it in the tray you baked it in.

4½ oz (130 g) smoked cream
   (see page 90)
1 large garlic clove, crushed
½ teaspoon salt
nutmeg and pepper, to taste
700 g potatoes, cut into
   ⅛ in (2 mm) thick slices

→ SERVES 4

Preheat the oven to 180°C/350°F/Gas mark 4. Line an oven dish 7 in square x 2 in deep (18 cm square x 5 cm deep) with baking paper.

Heat the cream, garlic and seasoning in a pan. The cream should taste salty because the potatoes are added with no seasoning. Add the potatoes to the cream and stir well. Place the mixture into the lined tray and press the potatoes down so they are all lying flat. Top with another sheet of baking paper.

Bake for 1 hour, or a little longer if needed. A knife should meet no resistance when piercing the potatoes.

Remove from the oven then place an equal-sized tray on top and place a weight (about 4 full beer bottles work well) into the tray and place all into the refrigerator until the dish is cool.

The next day preheat the oven to 200°C/400°F/Gas mark 6. Line a baking tray with baking paper.

Loosen the gratin from the sides of the dish with a knife and turn out onto a chopping board. Cut into squares.

Place the gratin squares onto the lined tray and bake for 15-20 minutes until heated through and lightly browned. Serve upside down as the base darkens nicely.

FRUIT SALAMI WITH AGED SMOKED CHEDDAR

This recipe is often a staple on cheese boards. It is easy to make, tasty and will last a couple of months in the refrigerator.

8 oz (1 cup/225 g) dried apricots
12 oz (2 cups/350 g) dried figs
6 oz (1 cup/175 g) dates
2 oz (½ cup/60 g) walnuts
4 tablespoons water
6 oz (1½ cups/175 g) icing (confectioners') sugar
zest of 1 orange
9 oz (250 g) smoked aged Cheddar (see page 89)

→ MAKES 2 X 8 IN (20 CM) ROLLS; 20 PORTIONS

Place all the fruit and nuts into a food processor and pulse to fine pieces.

Place the water, icing sugar and zest in a pan and boil to a light syrup. While still hot, add to the fruit in the processor and process until totally mixed in and a lump has formed.

On a clean work surface, divide the mixture in two and roll each into a sausage shape around 8 in (20 cm) long. Wrap in cling film (plastic wrap) and chill in the refrigerator.

Cut the rolls into thin discs and serve with aged smoked Cheddar.

ROAST APRICOTS WITH SMOKED MASCARPONE

This simple recipe works really well when fresh apricots are available. Roast apricots with thyme steeped in syrup is a great stand-alone dish but beautifully enhanced by the smoked mascarpone (see page 90). If you want to make your own mascarpone it is worth the time. A lovely simple dessert.

FOR THE ROAST APRICOTS
7 fl oz (200 ml) water
3 oz (90 g) caster (superfine) sugar
1 vanilla pod
8 apricots, halved
3 sprigs fresh thyme

smoked mascapone (see page 90)

→ SERVES 4

FOR THE ROAST APRICOTS

Preheat the oven to 200°C/400°F/Gas mark 6.

Place the water, sugar and vanilla in a pan and bring to the boil. Set aside.

Place the halved apricots on a roasting tray. Top with the thyme and roast until the apricots are lightly browned, 12-18 minutes. Remove from the oven, pour over the syrup and allow to cool.

Once cool, serve with the smoked mascarpone.

WARM SPICED PLUM TART WITH SMOKED WHITE CHOCOLATE ICE CREAM

This plum tart is a recipe that I made frequently while working in Switzerland. It's easy to substitute the plums with apples, apricots or peaches, if you like. The ground almonds (almond meal) help soak up any juice while baking.

FOR THE SMOKED WHITE CHOCOLATE ICE CREAM

8 fl oz (220 ml) milk
12 fl oz (350 ml) single (light) cream
1 vanilla pod (or 1 teaspoon vanilla extract)
3 egg yolks
1 tablespoon caster (superfine) sugar
5½ oz (160 g) white chocolate
5½ oz (160 g) smoked white chocolate (see page 88)

FOR THE PLUM TART

1 sheet sweet shortcrust pastry
2 tablespoons ground almonds (almond meal)
1 lb 2 oz (500 g) plums, pits removed and flesh quartered
¼ teaspoon ground cinnamon
¼ teaspoon ground mixed spice
⅛ teaspoon ground cloves
7 fl oz (200 ml) milk
3 eggs
1¾ oz (50 g) granulated (white) sugar

→ SERVES 6

FOR THE SMOKED WHITE CHOCOLATE ICE CREAM

In a large heavy pan bring the milk, cream and vanilla pod to a boil.

Whisk the egg yolks and sugar together in a bowl. While whisking, slowly pour in half the milk mixture, then whisk this back into the milk in the pan. Return to a medium heat and using a wooden spoon continuously stir until heated to 82°C/180°F, or until the mixture thickens enough to coat the back of the spoon.

Once cooked, place into a bowl and whisk in the white chocolate until all the chocolate has melted and is incorporated. Cool, then place into an ice cream machine and churn until frozen. Store the ice-cream in an airtight container in the freezer.

FOR THE PLUM TART

Preheat the oven to 150°C/300°F/Gas mark 2. Line an 8 x 8½ in (20 x 21 cm) baking tin (pan) with baking paper.

Line the base of the tin with the pastry, ensuring there are no holes and the sides are an even height. Sprinkle the almonds on the pastry then neatly place the plums over the base.

Mix together the remaining ingredients then lightly whisk to fully mix. Pour this mixture over the tart to just below the edge of the pastry.

Place the tray in the middle of the oven and bake for 55 minutes until the pastry is cooked and egg mixture is set.

Cool for 15 minutes and serve warm with smoked white chocolate ice cream. The tart is yummy served cold the following day!

SMOKING VEGETABLES & FRUIT

GIVE IT A GO! YOU WILL BE PLEASANTLY SURPRISED BY THE DELICIOUS RESULTS.

SMOKING VEGETABLES & FRUIT

When it comes to smoking vegetables and fruit there is no need to cure them beforehand. However, when hot smoking apples and pears, curing will help with the taste. I like to make up a little stock syrup and toss the apples or pears in this prior to smoking. It is also important to keep in mind the final use of the produce you are smoking and smoke only as long as you think necessary to avoid too strong a taste. A good rule of thumb is to start with a 30-minute smoke and taste the product being smoked to gauge it. Allow the product to stand for a couple of minutes before you try it to get a good idea of the strength of the smoke.

Vegetables and fruit can be either hot smoked or cold smoked depending on the final use. I've put together a basic guide of what vegetables and fruit are suitable for smoking. I tend to stay away from leafy greens such as spinach, bok choy (pak choi) or broccoli. If you would like a smoked finish with these types of vegetables I recommend adding smoked butter.

SUITABLE FOR HOT SMOKING:
ONIONS, EGGPLANT (AUBERGINE), JERUSALEM ARTICHOKES, PEARS, APPLES AND PINEAPPLES

SUITABLE FOR COLD SMOKING:
FENNEL BULBS, CAULIFLOWER, FIGS, STONE FRUITS

SUITABLE FOR BOTH:
TOMATOES, CAPSICUM (BELL PEPPERS), GARLIC, CORN ON THE COB (SWEETCORN), CHILLIES, MUSHROOMS, LEEKS

Remember that this is just a basic guide and that like many foods, vegetables and fruit can all be smoked in different ways and prepared with different seasonings.

I find hickory, maple and fruit woods work well with fruit and vegetables as these woods tend to be sweeter and not overly strong to taste.

HOT SMOKED SWEET POTATO

I enjoy the end result of smoking sweet potato (kumara), and it can be smoked alongside other items. Once smoked, treat it like you would unsmoked sweet potato.

2¼ lb (1 kg) whole golden sweet potato (kumara)

Use whatever wood you prefer. You will need enough for a 1-hour smoke.

Once the smoker is producing smoke, put the sweet potato in a tray and then place on a rack in the smoker and smoke for 1 hour. You want the chamber temperature at 80°C/176°F for the entire time.

HOT SMOKED CORN COBS

Leaving the cobs in the husks will help prevent them from drying out in the smoker. They will keep well in the refrigerator for a few days and can be used whenever you need cooked corn kernels in a recipe.

6 fresh corn cobs with husks
oil, for brushing
salt and pepper, to taste

I like to use hickory wood but use whatever you prefer. You will need enough wood or wood pellets for a 1-hour smoke.

Carefully peel back the corn husks, keeping them attached to the cob. Remove all the silky strands underneath.

To stop the corn from drying out and to help with the seasoning, pour enough water into a large bowl to soak the corn. Add 1 tablespoon (20 ml) of salt to every litre (2 teaspoons (10 ml) of salt to every pint) of water used. Stir until the salt has dissolved then soak the corn cobs with their husks attached for 1 hour.

Pat the corn cobs dry and lightly brush the corn with oil and season with salt and pepper. Gently pull the husks back over the cobs.

Once the smoker is producing smoke, place the cobs on a rack in the smoker and smoke for 1 hour ensuring the chamber temperature is 140°C/285°F for the entire time. Remove from the smoker and dehusk.

HOT SMOKED ONIONS

As onions are quite sweet they lend themselves well to being smoked.

4 large onions, peeled and sliced

I like to use apple wood but use whatever you prefer. You will need enough wood or wood pellets for a 1½-hour smoke.

Once the smoker is producing smoke, place the onions in a low-sided tray and put them in the smoker for 1½ hours. You want to achieve a chamber temperature around 80°C/176°F for the entire time.

Cool and store in an airtight container in the refrigerator for up to 2 weeks.

COLD SMOKED MUSHROOMS

After smoking, treat these as you would unsmoked mushrooms.

**12 medium field (portobello) mushrooms
salt and pepper, to taste**

Use whatever wood you prefer. You will need enough wood or wood pellets for a 1-hour smoke.

If necessary, clean the mushrooms by wiping them with paper towels.

Once the smoker is producing smoke, place the mushrooms on a tray or stainless rack and put them into the smoker for 1 hour, ensuring the chamber temperature is under 40°C/104°F the entire time.

Remove the tray and allow the mushrooms to cool. For storage, wrap in cling film (plastic wrap) and place in an airtight container in the refrigerator for up to 5 days.

COLD SMOKED BEETROOT

Beetroot is a wonderful vegetable to smoke; it helps turn something like a simple salad into a more complex dish with real taste and added shades of brown.

1 lb 6 oz (600 g) whole beetroot, peeled

I like to use maple or apple wood but use whatever you prefer. You will need enough wood or wood pellets for a 1-hour smoke.

Place the whole beetroot on a rack or a tray.

Once the smoker is producing smoke, place the whole beetroot into the smoker for 1 hour, ensuring the temperature in the chamber is less than 50°C/122°F the entire time the beetroot is in the smoker.

Remove and allow to cool. For storage, place in a airtight container in the refrigerator for up to 7 days.

COLD SMOKED TOMATOES

These are simple and tasty in salads, quiches or sauces. Adding a little sugar helps stop them becoming too bitter from the smoke.

20 vine-ripened tomatoes
olive oil, for brushing
salt and pepper, to taste
sugar, to taste

I like to use fruit woods or a blend for tomatoes but use whatever you prefer. You will need enough wood or wood pellets for a 30-minute smoke.

Slice the tomatoes in half, brush with a little oil, and season with the salt, pepper and sugar.

Once the smoker is producing smoke, place the tomato halves on a stainless steel rack in a tray and put them in the smoker for 30 minutes, ensuring the chamber temperature stays less than 30°C/85°F for the entire time.

Remove the tomatoes and allow them to cool. For storage, wrap in cling film (plastic wrap) and store in an airtight container in the refrigerator for up to 5 days.

Smoked tomatoes are best served at room temperature.

COLD SMOKED EGGPLANT

Smoking eggplant helps to bring alive this otherwise bland vegetable. When smoked it adds a real depth to dishes and purées.

3 eggplants (aubergines), cut into ⅜ in
 (1 cm) slices
salt and pepper, to taste
olive oil, for brushing

I like to use oak wood here but use whatever you prefer. You will need enough wood or wood pellets for a 1-hour smoke.

Season the eggplant with salt and pepper and allow to stand for 30 minutes. Pat the slices dry with paper towels and brush lightly with the oil.

Once the smoker is producing smoke, place the eggplant slices on a tray or stainless rack and put them into the smoker for 1 hour, ensuring the chamber temperature is less than 40°C/104°F for the entire time.

Remove the eggplant slices and allow them to cool. For storage, wrap in cling film (plastic wrap) and store in an airtight container in the refrigerator for up to 5 days.

COLD SMOKED PEARS

Smoked pears, once roasted, make a tasty winter dessert.

8 fl oz (250 ml/1 cup) apple juice
3 tablespoons butter
2 tablespoons liquid honey
1 vanilla pod (bean), split lengthways
2 cloves
4 pears, halved and cored

I like to use maple or apple wood but use whatever you prefer. You will need enough wood or wood pellets for a 1-hour smoke.

Place a small pan over a medium heat and combine the apple juice, butter, honey, vanilla pod and cloves. Cook to reduce to a syrup.

Place the pear halves in a low-sided tray then pour the apple syrup over the pears, coating them well.

Once the smoker is producing smoke, place the pear halves in the smoker for 1 hour, ensuring the chamber temperature remains less than 40°C/104°F. The pears are best roasted in the oven after smoking.

COLD SMOKED FIGS

Something a little different but very enjoyable, especially when used in salads.

8 ripe figs
maple syrup, for brushing

I like to use maple wood for figs but use whatever you prefer. You will need enough wood or wood pellets for a 30-minute smoke.

Slice the figs in half lengthways and with a pastry brush lightly coat the cut side of the figs with maple syrup.

Once the smoker is producing smoke, place the fig halves on a rack or a tray in the smoker for 30 minutes, ensuring the chamber temperature remains below 40°C/104°F for the entire time.

Remove the figs and allow to cool. Store in an airtight container in the refrigerator for up to 5 days.

SMOKED TOMATO CHUTNEY

I got the idea for this chutney from my good friend Craig, whose dad, Alan, makes a family-famous tomato chutney. My version uses smoked tomatoes and is a great addition to a number of dishes, giving them an individual touch. This chutney goes especially well with the grilled (broiled) chicken with smoked Brie and basil (see page 108).

vegetable oil, for cooking
2 onions, diced
5 Granny Smith apples, cored and diced
1 green capsicum (bell pepper), diced
2¼ lb (1 kg) cold smoked tomatoes (see page 124)
7 oz (1 cup/200 g) brown sugar
4 fl oz (½ cup/125 ml) red wine vinegar
5 oz (1 cup/150 g) raisins
salt and pepper, to taste

→ MAKES 6½ CUPS

Heat a large pan over a medium heat, add a little vegetable oil, then sauté the onions until transparent. Add the apples and capsicum and cook for a couple of minutes. Then add the smoked tomatoes, brown sugar, vinegar and raisins and cook over a low heat until the chutney thickens. Stir frequently to avoid the mixture sticking to the base of the pan.

After 60-75 minutes remove from the heat and season well with salt and pepper.

Store in sterilised jars or clean containers in the refrigerator for up to 6 weeks.

MEXICAN SMOKED CORN SALAD

I really enjoy this salad; the smokiness of the corn really makes it for me. It can be made without smoking the corn but it is well worth the time to do so. This is a great addition to any shared meal. It also tastes great when served with grilled (broiled) squid.

**6 hot smoked corn cobs
  (see page 121)
4 tablespoons olive oil
2 tablespoons red wine vinegar
salt and pepper, to taste
1 small red onion, finely diced
6 vine-ripened tomatoes, diced
1 small bunch fresh coriander
  (cilantro), chopped
1 red chilli, finely chopped**

→ **SERVES 4–6**

Remove the husks from the smoked corn cobs, along with any silky strands that may cling to the cob. Stand the cobs on a chopping board, slice the kernels from each cob, and place in a medium bowl.

In another bowl, whisk the oil and vinegar together, add the corn kernels and mix well.

Season to taste with salt and pepper, then add the onion, tomatoes, fresh coriander and chilli and gently mix together. Place into a serving bowl and serve warm.

SMOKED RATATOUILLE

You can use either smoked eggplants, courgettes or onions for the smoked ingredient in this dish. I like to use eggplants because they are easy to smoke and can be used in a few different recipes if you want to prepare a large batch. This dish goes particularly well with lamb, and I have also often served it with roast chicken or roast pork.

olive oil, for cooking
2 cold smoked eggplants
  (aubergines) (see page 124),
  finely diced
4 green courgettes (zucchini),
  finely diced
2 red capsicums (bell peppers),
  finely diced
1 onion, finely diced
2 sprigs fresh thyme
4 tablespoons tomato paste
2 tablespoons chopped basil
  leaves
salt and pepper, to taste

→ SERVES 4

Heat some olive oil in a large frying pan over a medium-high heat and sauté the diced eggplant until just cooked and lightly browned. Remove from the heat and place in a colander or strainer to drain any excess oil.

Repeat with the courgettes and capsicums.

Return the same pan to a medium heat, add some oil and sauté the onions until tender. Then add the thyme, cook for another 1 minute, then add the remaining ingredients and the sautéed eggplant, courgette and capsicum back into the pan. Combine and season to taste. Serve the ratatouille hot.

SMOKED SWEET POTATOES & BLUE CHEESE MASH

Sweet potato (kumara) is one of my choice vegetables to cook and eat. This recipe works equally well without smoking but the results using smoked sweet potato are worth the extra time. If you want to make a dairy-free version, cut out the blue cheese and add a touch more oil. It goes well with braised lamb shanks or slow-cooked oxtail or as a tasty addition to any barbecue.

2¼ lb (1 kg) hot smoked sweet potatoes (kumara) (see page 120)
3½ oz (100 g) blue cheese, diced
2 fl oz (60 ml) olive oil
salt and pepper, to taste

→ SERVES 4–6

Preheat the oven to 180°C/350°F/Gas mark 4.

Place the unpeeled sweet potatoes in the oven and bake for 50-60 minutes or until soft to the touch. To test if the sweet potatoes are cooked enough, pierce one with a small knife – there should be no resistance.

Remove from the oven and allow to stand for 5 minutes to cool, then peel the sweet potatoes and place them in a large bowl. Add the blue cheese and olive oil and season well with salt and pepper. Beat with a wooden spoon until the cheese and oil are incorporated. You can also do this in an cake mixer with a paddle attachment. Serve hot.

GRILLED EYE FILLET WITH SMOKED ONION PURÉE

I enjoy eye fillet (tenderloin). The smoked onion purée becomes the sauce for the meat and together with the eye fillet it makes a tasty meal. The purée is easy to make and has many uses, including under salads as a base, in beetroot salads, on pizzas, or served warm as a dip for smoked ribs.

For the smoked onion Purée
4 smoked onions (see page 121),
   sliced
oil, for cooking
salt and pepper, to taste
1¾ fl oz (50 ml) olive oil

→ **MAKES 2 CUPS**

FOR THE EYE FILLET
8 x 3½ oz (100 g) eye fillet
   (tenderloin) steaks
smoked sea salt (see page 153)
pepper
oil, for cooking
roasted tomatoes, to serve

→ **SERVES 4**

FOR THE SMOKED ONION PURÉE

Heat a pan over a low heat and add 1 teaspoon of oil and the onions. Cover the pan with a lid and cook the onions for about 1 hour until soft. Season well and purée until smooth in a blender while adding the olive oil. Adjust the seasoning and cool.

Store in an airtight container in the refrigerator for up to 2 weeks.

FOR THE EYE FILLET

Set the meat aside on the work surface for 30 minutes so it is at room temperature before cooking.

Season the meat well with the smoked salt and the pepper.

Heat a large heavy pan over a medium to high heat, add the oil until hot and then add the steaks. Cook the steaks for 3-4 minutes on each side then remove from the pan and set aside to rest for 3 minutes. Serve with smoked onion purée and roasted tomatoes.

SMOKED TOMATO & BASIL BRUSCHETTA

Tomatoes are one of the vegetables I most enjoy. I love their versatility, besides which they taste so good and with their bold tone they add presentation appeal to any dish. I often use them as a garnish; in fact it is something of a tradition for me to have a bowl of tomatoes within arm's reach while cooking! This dish is equally at home served as part of a long lazy Sunday lunch or light snack, depending on your mood.

2 garlic cloves, halved
12 slices ciabatta
olive oil, for brushing
20 cold smoked vine-ripened
  tomatoes (see page 124),
  halved
1 red onion, finely sliced
1 small bunch fresh basil,
  gently ripped
balsamic vinegar, to taste
salt and pepper, to taste

→ SERVES 6

Preheat the grill (broiler) to 180°C/350°F.

Rub the garlic halves on one side of each slice of bread. Brush the same side of the bread slices with olive oil and grill (broil) until lightly browned.

Mix the tomato halves, red onions and half the basil leaves in a large bowl. Then add some olive oil, balsamic vinegar and salt and pepper to taste.

Evenly divide the mixture between the grilled ciabatta slices, top with the remaining basil and serve.

SMOKED MUSHROOM TARTS

This tart recipe is a little different from the traditional one you might expect. These are very easy to make and can be made to look very attractive. This very useful entrée dish can be mostly prepared and put together at the last minute.

2 sheets puff pastry
oil, for brushing
salt
12 medium smoked field
  (portobello) mushrooms (see
  page 122), sliced
1 sprig fresh thyme
salt and pepper, to taste
12 tablespoons smoked onion
  purée (see page 134)
4 oz (120 g) feta, crumbled
4 teaspoons balsamic reduction
  (see page 152)
4 teaspoons olive oil
small salad leaves, for garnish

→ SERVES 6

Preheat the oven to 200°C/400°F/Gas mark 6. Line a large baking tray with baking paper.

Cut each pastry sheet into 6 rectangles. Place the rectangles on the lined tray, brush with a little oil and sprinkle with a little salt. Cover the pastry with another sheet of baking paper and place a cake rack upside down on top to weigh them down.

Bake for 12 minutes, or until golden brown. Remove from the oven and allow the pastry to cool on a cake rack.

Heat a large frying pan to medium to high, add a little oil and fry the mushrooms until lightly browned. Then add the thyme and season well with salt and pepper. Set aside.

Assemble the tarts while the mushrooms and cases are still warm. Spread the onion purée on each case, top with the mushrooms and sprinkle on the feta. Dress each tart with the balsamic reduction and olive oil, and garnish with baby salad leaves. Serve warm.

FALAFEL WITH SMOKED EGGPLANT PURÉE

These falafel are best served with pitta bread and a little salad of grated (shredded) carrots, cucumber and lettuce. Top with the smoked eggplant purée for a tasty lunch.

FOR THE SMOKED EGGPLANT PURÉE
3 cold smoked eggplants (aubergines) (see page 124)
2 garlic cloves, thinly sliced
1 sprig thyme
3 tablespoons olive oil
2 tablespoons tahini
1 tablespoon lemon juice
½ bunch flat-leaf parsley
salt and pepper, to taste

FOR THE FALAFEL
1 x 14 oz (400 g) can chickpeas, drained
1 small red onion, diced
3 garlic cloves
1¾ oz (50 g) rice flour
¼ teaspoon ground coriander
¼ teaspoon ground fennel seeds
½ teaspoon paprika
1 tablespoon chopped parsley
1 tablespoon chopped coriander
salt and pepper, to taste
oil, for cooking

TO SERVE
fresh coriander (cilantro), to garnish

→ SERVES 2–3

FOR THE PURÉE
Preheat the oven to 180°C/350°F/Gas mark 4. Line a baking tray with aluminium foil.

Place the sliced eggplant on the foil and top with the garlic, thyme and 2 tablespoons of the olive oil.

Roast in the oven for 15 minutes then cover with aluminium foil and bake for another 20-30 minutes, or until soft.

Place the roasted eggplant, remaining olive oil, tahini, lemon juice and parsley in a blender and purée until smooth. Season well with salt and pepper.

FOR THE FALAFEL
Place the chickpeas, onion, garlic, rice flour and spices in a food processor and purée until fine, add the fresh herbs and pulse until combined, then season with salt and pepper.

Scoop out heaped tablespoons of the mixture and form into small discs. Heat a large frying pan over a medium heat, add a little cooking oil then fry the falafel for a few minutes on each side until golden brown. Drain on paper towels and keep warm. Repeat until all the falafel are cooked.

TO SERVE
Place a little eggplant purée on each falafel and garnish with fresh coriander.

SMOKED BEETROOT SALAD

A great salad to serve at a barbecue or as part of a shared meal. This classic combination is often seen in restaurants although it is also simple and easy for you to make and enjoy yourself.

FOR THE ROASTED SMOKED BEETROOT

1 lb 6 oz (600 g) whole smoked beetroot (see page 122)
2 fl oz (¼ cup/60 ml) olive oil
2 tablespoons liquid honey
2 tablespoons red wine vinegar
salt and pepper, to taste

TO ASSEMBLE

1 pear, core removed and thinly sliced
2 large handfuls rocket (arugula) leaves
4 small vine-ripened tomatoes, cut into wedges
3½ oz (100 g) goat's cheese, crumbled
6 dried figs, thinly sliced
2 oz (60 g) vinaigrette (see page 152)
salt and pepper, to taste

➜ SERVES 4–6

FOR THE ROASTED SMOKED BEETROOT

Preheat the oven to 180°C/350°F/Gas mark 4. Line an oven tray with baking paper.

Cut each beetroot into 8 wedges.

Mix together the olive oil, honey and red wine vinegar in a bowl, and season with salt and pepper. Add the wedges of beetroot and coat well. Place on the lined tray and roast until tender, 35-40 minutes. Test with a small knife - there should be no resistance.

Allow to cool before using. For storage, place in an airtight container in the refrigerator for 5-7 days.

TO ASSEMBLE

Place the beetroot on a large serving plate. Combine the remaining ingredients in a large bowl and gently mix together. Scatter this mixture over the beetroot. Serve immediately.

SMOKED FIG, ROCKET & ITALIAN FRIED BREAD SALAD WITH RED WINE REDUCTION

This salad is a great way to use fresh figs when the season begins. Lightly grill the figs before using to warm them through – this is a nice touch to enhance the dish.

FOR THE ITALIAN FRIED BREAD
1 level teaspoon active dried yeast
5½ fl oz (160 ml) tepid water
10½ oz (300 g) strong white bread flour
⅔ oz (20 g) lard or butter
½ teaspoon salt
canola oil, for deep-frying
salt, to taste

TO ASSEMBLE
10½ oz (300 g) rocket (arugula) leaves
1 pear, cored and thinly sliced
4–5 tablespoons vinaigrette (see page 152)
8 cold smoked figs (see page 125), halved
16–20 Italian fried bread strips
1¾ oz (50 g) Parmesan, shaved
2 tablespoons olive oil
1 tablespoon red wine reduction (see page 152)

→ SERVES 4

FOR THE ITALIAN FRIED BREAD

Place the yeast and water in a bowl and leave for 5 minutes.

Place the flour on the work surface, make a well in the centre and add the lard and salt. Slowly add the water while using your hands to form a dough. Knead the dough for 6-8 minutes.

Place the dough in a bowl, cover with cling film (plastic wrap) and allow to stand in a warm place for 1½-2 hours until doubled in size.

Dust the work surface with a little flour and roll out the dough to ¼ in (5-6 mm) thickness. Cut into strips 1¼ x 4 in (3 x 10 cm) long.

Heat 2 in (5 cm) of oil in a pan to 175°C/350°F and fry the dough strips in batches until golden brown on each side. Drain on paper towels and season with salt.

TO ASSEMBLE

Place the rocket leaves and pear slices in a large bowl and dress with the vinaigrette, tossing the leaves gently.

Place the figs on the serving plate, add the fried bread strips, top with the rocket and pears, and scatter on the Parmesan. Finish by drizzling over the olive oil and red wine reduction.

SMOKED PEARS WITH CINNAMON CREAM

This is a delicious way to enjoy winter pears.

**4 cold smoked pears
  (see page 125), halved**

FOR THE CINNAMON CREAM
**¼ pint (150 ml) single (light)
  cream**
**2 tablespoons icing
  (confectioners') sugar**
¼ teaspoon ground cinnamon
2 drops vanilla extract

→ **SERVES 4**

Preheat the oven to 160°C/325°F/Gas mark 3.

Bake the pears until soft, 30-40 minutes. Test with a small knife - there should be no resistance.

FOR THE CINNAMON CREAM

Place the cream in a bowl with the sugar, cinnamon and vanilla. Whip until soft peaks form.

Place the pears on a large serving tray, and using a hot spoon dollop cream onto each pear. Serve immediately.

BASICS

GARLIC DRESSING

→ MAKES 1 PINT (600 ML)

2 egg yolks
3 tablespoons wine wine vinegar
2 tablespoons Dijon mustard
3–4 garlic cloves
14 fl oz (400 ml) canola oil
3½ fl oz (100 ml) olive oil
2 oz (60 g) Parmesan
salt and pepper, to taste
2 tablespoons chopped flat-leaf parsley

Process the egg yolks, vinegar, mustard and garlic in a food processor.

With the speed set to high, slowly drizzle in the oils until the mixture forms an emulsion. If the mixture becomes too thick, add a little water to thin. Once all the oil has been added, blend in the Parmesan and season with salt and pepper. Lightly stir the parsley into the dressing.

Store in an airtight container in the refrigerator for up to 4 weeks.

CAPER MAYONNAISE

→ MAKES 8 FL OZ (1 CUP/250 ML)

2 egg yolks
1 tablespoon wholegrain mustard
1 tablespoon white wine vinegar
8 fl oz (1 cup/250 ml) canola oil
2 tablespoons capers, drained and chopped
2 tablespoons chopped gherkins
1 tablespoon chopped parsley
salt and pepper, to taste

Put the egg yolks, mustard and vinegar into a medium bowl and whisk together well. While whisking continuously, slowly drizzle in the oil until an emulsion forms and all the oil has been used. Add the remaining ingredients and season with salt and pepper.

Store in an airtight container in the refrigerator for up to 4 weeks.

LEMON AÏOLI

→ MAKES 8 FL OZ (1 CUP/250 ML)

2 egg yolks
2 garlic cloves, finely crushed
1 tablespoon wholegrain mustard
1 teaspoon white wine vinegar
8 fl oz (1 cup/250 ml) grapeseed oil
1 tablespoon lemon juice
salt and pepper, to taste

Put the egg yolks, garlic, mustard and vinegar into a medium bowl and whisk together well.

While whisking continuously, slowly drizzle in the oil until an emulsion forms and all the oil has been used.

Whisk in the lemon juice and season well with salt and pepper.

Store in an airtight container in the refrigerator for up to 4 weeks.

APPLE CHUTNEY

→ MAKES 3½ CUPS

2 tablespoons oil
7 oz (200 g) red onions, diced
1¾ lb (800 g) cooking apples, peeled and diced
2½ fl oz (75 ml) water
3½ fl oz (110 ml) red wine vinegar
¼ teaspoon ground ginger
½ teaspoon salt
1 teaspoon mustard powder
¼ teaspoon ground cloves
¼ teaspoon ground five spice
4½ oz (125 g) brown sugar
4½ oz (125 g) prunes, diced

Heat the oil in a large pan over a medium heat, add the onions and sauté for a couple of minutes, then add the remaining ingredients. Gently cook for 60-75 minutes, or until the liquid has reduced and the mixture thickened. Stir frequently to avoid the chutney sticking to the base of the pan.

Cool, then place in an airtight container and store in the refrigerator for 3-4 weeks.

BARBECUE SAUCE

→ MAKES 3½ CUPS

oil, for cooking
1 onion, diced
4 garlic cloves, crushed
¼ teaspoon celery seeds
8 fl oz (1 cup/250 ml) tomato sauce
8 fl oz (1 cup/250 ml) tomato juice
4 fl oz (½ cup/125 ml) liquid honey
4 fl oz (½ cup/125 ml) water cider vinegar
2 fl oz (¼ cup/60 ml) mild English mustard
2 tablespoons Tabasco sauce
2 tablespoons Worcestershire sauce
2 tablespoons sweet smoked paprika
salt and pepper, to taste

Heat a large pan over a medium heat and add a little oil. Sauté the onions and garlic in the oil until soft. Add the celery seeds and cook for another 1 minute. Add the remaining ingredients and bring to the boil. Simmer until thickened, about 20 minutes. Season with salt and pepper.

Transfer to a food processor and purée until smooth.

Use immediately or store in an airtight container in the refrigerator for up to 4 weeks.

BALSAMIC OR RED WINE REDUCTION

→ MAKES 2 FL OZ (50–60 ML)

This simple reduction can be made by following the recipe or, to make a red wine reduction, simply replace the balsamic vinegar with all red wine for a sweeter result.

3½ fl oz (100 ml) balsamic vinegar
3½ fl oz (100 ml) red wine
1 oz (30 g) brown sugar

Place all the ingredients in a pan and simmer until the liquid has reduced to 2 fl oz (50–60 ml) and is the consistency of a thin syrup. It will thicken more on cooling. Take care not to reduce the liquid too much or the reduction may burn.

VINAIGRETTE

→ MAKES 6 FL OZ (175 ML)

1 tablespoon wholegrain mustard
½ teaspoon sugar
½ teaspoon salt
1 ½ fl oz (40 ml) red wine vinegar
¼ pint (150 ml) grapeseed oil

Place the mustard, sugar, salt and vinegar into a bowl and whisk together.

While continuously whisking, slowly drizzle in the canola oil until incorporated.

Store in an airtight container in the refrigerator for up to 2 weeks.

COLD SMOKED SEA SALT

You can make this while smoking other products if you want to fill up the smoking chamber.

1 x 9 oz (250 g) packet flaky sea salt

I like to use apple wood but use whatever you prefer. You will need enough wood or wood pellets for a 3-hour smoke.

Place the salt onto a tray and spread it out evenly.

When the smoker is producing smoke, place the salt into the smoker and cold smoke for up to 3 hours, depending on how strong you want the taste to be. Ensure the chamber temperature remains less than 40°C/104°F for the entire time.

If the salt is a little wet after the smoking, place into an oven at 70°C/150°F and dry out, for about 1 hour.

RUB #1

6 tablespoons flaky sea salt
2 tablespoons sweet smoked paprika
4 tablespoons brown sugar
1 teaspoon ground black pepper
2 teaspoons dried oregano
1 teaspoon dried basil

Combine all the ingredients and use as required. Or store in an airtight container for up to 1 month.

RUB #2

6 tablespoons flaky sea salt
3 tablespoons sweet smoked paprika
4 tablespoons brown sugar
1 teaspoon ground black pepper
2 teaspoons cayenne pepper
1 teaspoon garlic powder
1 teaspoon onion powder
1 teaspoon dried basil

Combine all the ingredients and use as required. Store in an airtight container for up to 1 month.

CROUTONS

4 slices white bread, diced into fingernail-size cubes
1¾ oz (50 g) butter
2½ fl oz (75 ml) grapeseed oil
salt, to taste

Heat a frying pan large enough to hold all the bread cubes over a medium heat.

Add the oil and butter, and once the butter is melted add the diced bread. Gently cook while lightly stirring until all the bread is golden brown.

Line a colander with paper towels and tip the croutons on the towels to drain. Season with salt.

Store in an airtight container for up to 2 days.

➡ GLOSSARY

AGAR AGAR a setting agent made from seaweed, available in powder or flakes

ARANCINI OR ARANCINE fried rice balls coated with breadcrumbs (from Italy)

BEEF EYE OF ROUND a tenderloin steak cut from the round of the rear leg of beef; available from your butcher

BLINI a yeasted pancake traditionally made with buckwheat flour in Russia

BRISKET a cut that is taken from the breast section of beef or veal

CIABATTA a chewy, crusty white Italian loaf bread

GARLIC POWDER dry powdered garlic found in the spice section of the supermarket or bulk food store

MANUKA WOOD sometimes known as Tea tree (*Leptospermum scoparium*). A myrtle tree native to New Zealand and South East Australia.

PARMESAN a tasty Italian hard cheese

PINK CURING SALT also known as Prague powder or Colorquik: the mix is dyed pink so as not to be confused with plain salt. It's a mix of around 94 per cent salt and 6 per cent nitrite. Pink curing salt is highly poisonous – check the instructions on the packet for safe handling of this product

SLIDER a sandwich served in a small bread bun

SNAPPER or Schnapper (*Chrysophrys auratus*). A large fish common in southern hemisphere coastal waters, elsewhere sometimes known as bream

TONGUE generally beef or veal, it is similar in taste to brisket and corned beef

85vl a visual measure (visually lean) of the proportion of fat to lean meat e.g. 85vl meat should have 15 per cent fat

TROUBLESHOOTING TIPS

FAULT	POSSIBLE REASON	CORRECTION
too pale	not dry enough/too wet not smoked long enough	dry longer before smoking smoke longer
too dark	smoked too long too hot	shorter smoke time cooler smoke
product too bitter	not enough sugar in cure smoked too long	add more sugar shorten smoke time

 # STOCKISTS & SUPPLIERS

SMOKERS & SMOKING UNITS

Bradley Smoker www.bradleysmoker.com

Smokai www.smokai.com

SPECIALTY INGREDIENTS & EQUIPMENT

United States: Walton's Inc. www.waltonsinc.com

United Kingdom and Europe: Arden Smoker Supplies www.foodsmoker.co.uk

Australia: Orange Farm Hardware www.orangefarmhardware.com.au

MEASURING GUIDE

ABBREVIATIONS

g	gram
kg	kilogram
mm	millimetre
cm	centimetre
ml	millilitre
°C/°F	degrees Celsius/Fahrenheit
oz	ounces
fl oz	fluid ounces

WEIGHT CONVERSIONS

The closest equivalent imperial measurement is given for each metric measurement.

IMPERIAL	METRIC
½ oz	15 g
1 oz (= 28 g more exactly)	30 g
3½ oz	100 g
5 oz	150 g
7 oz	200 g
9 oz	250 g
14 oz	400 g
16 oz (1 lb)	450 g
1 lb 2 oz	500 g
36 oz (2¼ lb)	1 kg

CUP AND SPOON CONVERSIONS

SPOON/CUP	METRIC
½ teaspoon	2.5 ml
1 teaspoon	5 ml
1 tablespoon	15 ml
¾ cup	175 ml (6 fl oz)
1 cup	250 ml (8 fl oz)
1½ cups	375 ml (13 fl oz)
2 cups	500 ml (17 fl oz)
4 cups	1 litre (1 ¾ pints)

LIQUID CONVERSIONS—GENERAL

IMPERIAL	METRIC
⅙ fl oz	5 ml
½ fl oz	15 ml
1 fl oz (= 28 ml more exactly)	30 ml
3½ fl oz	100 ml
4 fl oz	125 ml
5 fl oz (¼ pint imperial)	150 ml
7 fl oz	200 ml
8 fl oz	225 ml
9 fl oz	250 ml
16 fl oz	450 ml
17 fl oz	500 ml
36 fl oz (1¾ pint imperial,	1 litre

OVEN TEMPERATURES

	CELSIUS	FAHRENHEIT	GAS MARK
very cool	110°C	225°F	¼
	120°C	250°F	½
cool	140°C	275°F	1
	150°C	300°F	2
moderate	170°C	325°F	3
	180°C	350°F	4
moderate-hot	190°C	375°F	5
	200°C	400°F	6
hot	220°C	425°F	7
	230°C	450°F	8
very hot	240°C	475°F	9

MINCER-PLATE SIZES

4 mm	⅛ inch	fine
6 mm	¼ inch	medium
9 mm	⅜ inch	coarse

INDEX

First published in 2014 by New Holland Publishers Pty Ltd

London • Sydney • Auckland

The Chandlery Unit 009 50 Westminster Bridge Road London SE1 7QY United Kingdom

1/66 Gibbes Street Chatswood NSW 2067 Australia

218 Lake Road Northcote Auckland New Zealand

www.newhollandpublishers.com

A record of this book is held at the British Library and the National Library of Australia.

ISBN 9781742576381

Publishing manager: Christine Thomson
Editor: Rebecca Lal
Design: Athena Sommerfeld
Author photograph: Devin Hart

Front cover image: Hot smoked salmon
Back cover images, from top to bottom: Warm spiced plum tart with smoked white chocolate ice-cream; smoked egg & lamb's lettuce salad; smoked potato gratin.

Printer: Toppan Leefung Printing Limited, China

10 9 8 7 6 5 4 3 2 1

Keep up with New Holland Publishers on Facebook
www.facebook.com/NewHollandPublishers

The recipes in this book have been carefully tested by the author. The publishers and the author have made every effort to ensure that the recipes and instructions pertaining to them are accurate and safe but cannot accept liability for any resulting injury or loss or damage to property whether direct or consequential.

WARNING: It is crucial to make sure that all equipment is very clean and cold when making sausages or cured meats. After making sausages, wash the equipment and before reusing it, check to make sure you have not missed anything the first time. When smoking food, be aware that all smokers are different, and it is likely there will be some variance in the smoke food taste, which can be adjusted by shortening or lengthening the smoking time.